OVERVIEW

Do you know how chakras, yoga, and essential oils can help student athletes achieve optimal performance levels? What advice would you give your student athlete on how to approach a coach when conflict arises? Do you know what to consider in selecting a sports league for your child? Have you ever wondered what more you can do to get the best recovery results for your child after an injury? Do you need some real insight into the college recruiting world?

Most Valuable Parents: A Guide for Parents of Student Athletes has insight into these hot topics of discussion and so much more. It is a masterfully composed, comprehensive resource for parents of student athletes – any level, every sport.

It is a journey that will educate, empower, and enlighten parents of student athletes as they support their children's sports endeavors. Whether you are a first time parent of a student athlete or a seasoned parent with more than one student athlete, it will be thought provoking and impactful. It will easily become an invaluable reference for Most Valuable Parents everywhere.

Dedicated To:

Danielle and Devin

My Heart and My Strength!

It has been my absolute pleasure to share in your journeys as

student athletes.

I have treasured every priceless moment and

look forward to creating many more special memories.

I am so proud of each of you and your accomplishments.

I am inspired by your caring spirits, determination, and tenacity on and
off the court.

You are both the manifestation of all of the good in your Dad and I. I
pray supernatural blessings over your lives!

I love you both eternally and

I will be "Team Danielle" and "Team Devin" all the way!

INTRODUCTION

Parents of student athletes are a different breed. We are chauffeurs and dispatchers— coordinating rides for early morning practices and late night games. We are snack preparers and short order chefs for our student athletes that are burning calories at the speed of light and therefore ALWAYS, ALWAYS hungry. We are prayer warriors, spiritual advisors, and counselors--when our children need words of encouragement, guidance, or just need a sounding board. We are Team Moms/Team Dads coordinating the needs for the team. We are concession stand workers and cheering squads. We are nurses and therapists when our children are injured and we are trying to make sure the doctor's orders are followed. We are ATM machines paying for athletic gear, club fees, admission costs for tournaments, hotel expenses, letterman jackets, and so much more. Basically, we are whatever we need to be to support our children's sports endeavors.

We salute each and every parent of a student athlete and this book is dedicated to Most Valuable Parents everywhere! This unique and comprehensive guide covers a range of topics for parents of student athletes of any sport- at every level. Whether you are a first time parent of a student athlete or a seasoned parent with several student athletes— you will discover valuable information that you can use throughout your journey as Most Valuable Parents!

CHAPTER 1

THE "WONDER YEARS":
Building an Athletic Foundation During the Early Years

Playing sports plant seeds for greatness and its immeasurable benefits can be reaped throughout a lifetime. It promotes health and physical fitness; provides lessons in discipline and leadership; instills confidence; and teaches resilience, mental toughness, and so much more! The early experience of playing sports will teach your children how to celebrate wins and how to handle losses. Perhaps the best perks of all are the sheer fun and the priceless camaraderie!

Parents, encourage your children to explore as many different sports as possible during their early childhood years, "The Wonder Years." Go ahead—allow your children to flex those little muscles. Whether it's football, basketball, soccer, gymnastics, swimming, volleyball, cheerleading/ dance, karate, tennis, golf, lacrosse, rugby, or track and field—your children should be encouraged to experiment with as many sports as they have an opportunity.

Exposing children to a variety of sports in their early childhood can prove to have many benefits, as it will create a solid foundation to build upon. During these "Wonder Years" everyone usually gets playing time and referees and coaches often take more time to explain game rules and correct forms and techniques. Also, during these formative years, having fun is prioritized! Furthermore, children and parents are able to experiment to determine what sport is the best fit for their children's personalities and physical abilities. Playing multiple sports can also foster and improve your children's skills in other sports. For instance, running track may improve a football player's speed on the field, or playing soccer can enhance a player's skills on the basketball court. Former NBA players Steve Nash and Kobe Bryant have attributed their vision on a basketball court to playing soccer in their youth. Besides, single sport-specialization too early can cause a child to burnout on a particular sport and can increase the risk of injury due to overused muscles.

As children grow older we must consider their personal motivation, skill level, and passion in determining when or if it's the right time to specialize in a sport. If your child truly wants to compete on an elite level and exhibits the physical ability to do so-eventually they may have to specialize. Schedules become more hectic, training and practices are more intense, financial commitments become greater, games become more competitive, and the overall sacrifices with time invested become real for student athletes and parents. In the rare instance your child demonstrates the ability to balance and excel at more than one sport and the financial and scheduling commitments can be met— a student athlete may opt to play more than one sport on an elite level. Every circumstance is unique and parents should help their children carefully analyze the pros and cons for their particular circumstances.

Parents you should recognize that you may be biased towards a sport you played in your youth, or maybe you are just a fan of watching a particular sport. It is only natural for you to favor that particular sport over other sports. You may feel you can teach your children more because you have more insight and experience with a particular sport or that you will bond better if they choose your favorite sport. There is nothing wrong with parents wanting their children to play the sport they played as a child. However, parents you must keep in mind each child is a unique individual. Although children carry their parents' DNA— children still have their own unique physical traits, personalities, and interests. In other words, "Little John" may not ever grow taller than 5' 2" and may never develop a true love for the game of basketball. It does not matter if "Big John" led his high school team to a State Championship 20 years ago. Whatever sport your children eventually pick as their sport(s) of choice, should be your child's choice. Influence from the parent is fine, but the decision should still be your child's decision. You do not want your child to grow up to resent the sport or you because their heart was never truly in it.

CHAPTER 2
WHEN YOU KNOW BETTER, YOU DO BETTER:
Health, Safety, Personal Care and More

Have you ever got a whiff of a student athlete after practice and the body odor was so strong it made your eyes burn? Have you ever seen a kid get scratched down to the white meat during a game by another player with claw-like nails? Have you ever seen a child get a tooth knocked out or loosened during a sporting event? Have you ever heard a child complain of chest pains? Have you ever witnessed a child engage in under aged drinking or drug use? Have you ever watched a child arrive to practice late and skip warming up? Do you know if your school gym has a defibrillator, and if so —where is it located? Do any of these questions cause you to raise an eyebrow and nod in agreement or scratch your head? If so, do not be alarmed just become aware.

Parents be reminded, our student athletes are still developing and learning good habits throughout their childhood. Oftentimes, they are super busy and may not prioritize those little things we know are important. As parents, we just assume our children know better. Sometimes they do, but sometimes their judgement might be questionable. Parents take time to review some of the basics with your children to make sure they understand and prioritize their health, safety, and personal care. The following addresses some of these basics and provides some additional tidbits of information that every parent of a student athlete should also know.

PHYSICAL EXAMINATIONS
One of the keys to ensure your student athlete has the safest experience possible while playing sports is to be proactive. Many school districts require all athletes complete a physical exam annually. It is commonly called a Pre-Participation Physical Exam. This is perhaps one of the most important things a parent can do for their children even if it is NOT

a requirement. These exams can help detect conditions that may limit or restrict a student's ability to play in sports safely. Parents you should take these tests seriously. The usual test consists of checking height, weight, blood pressure, pulse, vision, heart, lungs, abdomen, ears, and throat. During these exams, they also evaluate your child's posture, joints, strength and flexibility. Parents you may even consider taking an extra step and request an electrocardiogram for your student athletes (EKG). EKGs monitor the electrical signals that control how the heart beats and pumps blood. This is a non-invasive test that may detect unknown congenital heart conditions in children. Parents, knowledge of your children's condition can help you make the best decisions concerning their health while playing sports. Children can be tested at your local pediatricians' offices, clinics, and even urgent care facilities. Oftentimes the schools will post locations of facilities around the community that host exams after hours or even on the weekend for your convenience.

PRE-EXISTING CONDITIONS
Maintaining good health for children with pre-existing conditions is very important. Encourage your children to be responsible and to commit to taking medication as required or as needed. For example, children with asthma should keep their inhalers on them at all times. It should be as second nature to them as making sure they bring their game shoes.

LISTEN TO YOUR BODY
Another thing parents should do to promote good health is to encourage their children to pay attention to their bodies and tell someone if they are experiencing any frequent and unusual issues i.e., shortness of breath, chest pains, chronic pains, and dizziness. Your children must learn to exercise good judgement and understand the importance of listening to their body's warning signs rather than fearing loss of playing time. Parents we must have these important conversations with our children. It is not a sign of weakness to know your body's limitations. I tell my children all the time, "You have only one body assigned to you. Fifty

years from now, with cloning possibilities, that may change. Right now, you have one body that you must take care of for the rest of your life." With that said, they must learn to decipher between playing through pain verses playing through injury; being a little exhausted verses being severely dehydrated; and listening to their own voice of reason verses ignoring their gut. I am a fan of pushing one's limits –that is how a student athlete will stretch, grow stronger, and get better. I am not talking about being a little fatigued or having little aches and pains, I am talking about those big red flags that might feel very unusual and should never be ignored. The more experienced children become engaging in sports activities, the more in tune they will become with their own bodies. Teach them early to pay attention to their bodies and speak up if they feel something is off. It is always better to err on the side of caution.

STRETCHING

Every student athlete should know how to properly stretch at all levels of play. When muscles are warm and stretched, movements become easier and more fluid-like. This helps prevent injuries. It is imperative that children incorporate stretching as part of their regimen before each practice and every game -no exceptions.

PROTECTIVE GEAR

Parents make sure your children have their proper safety gear and make sure they actually wear it. Statistics show children are injured at a higher rate during practices as opposed to during actual games. Encourage your children to wear safety gear at all times to minimize the risk of injury.

We all know that there is a lot of fancy stuff out there on the market classified as "protective gear." We understand your children may want to rock a certain swag when they play sports. There is a lot to choose from and it can add up quickly in cost. Parents, consider shopping for sports equipment out of season or look for deals online. Do not worry so much about the brand and style just make sure the item is functional and of good quality (especially those items that will NOT be visible anyway). Remember the ultimate goal is to minimize the risk of injury to your child. Real swag is a state of mind and not a brand on their gear. They can show their swag on the court or field during game time.

Some equipment is mandatory to play a sport and some accessories are optional. I implore every parent to do your own research and invest in good protective gear for your student athletes. Each sport may require specific gear and there may be new and improved stuff on the market each season. If your child is new to a sport pay attention to other athletes, talk to other parents and coaches, check reviews and then determine what is best for your child.

Make sure any accessories worn are within the league's regulations. Usually teams will provide you with standard equipment. However, optional gear and accessories (i.e. protective pads, shin guards, jock straps, knee pads, mouth pieces, special footwear, and other safety gear) could ensure your children are less likely to suffer injuries or re-injuries.

There are some impressive products on the market. One being, the Zamst A2-DX Ankle brace, which is bar none one of the best high performance ankle braces on the market. Another impressive product is the Shock Doctor's protective mouth guard. It is reasonably priced and offers an actual dental warranty. If a person suffers dental damage while wearing their guard, they will extend dental coverage. Again, take the time to do your own research to determine what protective products are the best fit for your child's needs.

Minimizing the risk of injury or severity of an injury is the ultimate goal. Ensuring your student athletes are using protective gear may be half the battle. Parents be sure their gear is appropriately sized and is in good condition, especially if using hand-me-downs from older siblings. The wrong sized gear may not be effective and could prove to be harmful. Shoes wear out and lose their grip; pads wear down and become thin;

and straps may loosen and break. Make it a point to inspect your children's gear and replace as needed.

HYGIENE

Hygiene should not be taken for granted as good hygiene is critical in promoting health and safety. Teach your student athlete good hygiene early. Parents warn your children of the hidden dangers of poor hygiene so they will learn to take the necessary precautions to prevent viral infections (e.g., cold and flu), bacterial infections (e.g., MRSA, strep throat), fungal infections (e.g., ringworms, athlete's foot) and even infections with parasites (e.g., scabies and lice).

Here are some basics every student athlete should know:
- Wash your hands often and thoroughly with warm water and soap. Use sanitizer if soap and water are not available.
- Do not share personal items. Avoid sharing towels, brushes, combs, make-up etc.
- Shower thoroughly and clean your body ASAP after games. Shampoo your hair regularly. Use antibacterial soap.
- Trim your nails. Scratches in contact sports are common.
- Cover your wounds to prevent infections.
- Protect your feet. Athlete's foot is real, and funky feet are embarrassing. Avoid damp socks and tightly fitted shoes. Wash and dry your feet thoroughly and do not forget to dry between your toes. Consider using foot powder if sweaty feet are an issue.
- Wash your clothes and uniforms regularly.
- Wear proper undergarments. Breathable cotton, loose fitted underwear can prevent yeast infections with girls and jock itch with boys.
- Never share drinks. The easiest way to pass germs is through sharing drinks. At the very least, use the "waterfall method".
- If you have a fever or contagious ailments like strep or pink eye, let the coach know and quarantine yourself throughout the recommended period you are contagious. No need in taking out the whole team.

DRUGS/ALCOHOL

There is a real good reason drug use is illegal and children are not legally allowed to consume alcohol. One being, our children are still in the process of developing good judgment. An adolescent's use of alcohol and/or drugs can have disastrous consequences. Although there are many news stories of documented tragedies involving our youth and the use of drugs and alcohol –it remains a problem.

Student athletes may make the choice to use drugs and alcohol for various reasons: to relax and/or be social, to gain a competitive edge, to have more energy to keep up with their demanding schedules, and/or to suppress pain from an actual injury. Whatever the reason, they may feel it is justified in that moment or they may feel it is NOT a big deal. Parents, you must impress upon your children that there may be serious, irrevocable consequences drug/alcohol use can have in their lives (i.e., legal ramifications, compromise of academic and athletic standing, health issues, and/or personal shame to everything they have worked so hard to accomplish). Help your children understand they are NOT invincible and tragedy and misfortune from the use of drinking and drug use has no restriction on age. Parents it is worth having a conversation about underage drinking and drug use with your student athlete no matter how cliché it may seem.

You can easily open the conversation by discussing events in the news. Here are some fictitious headliners that are based on actual news stories and events that can serve as icebreakers.

"A 17-year-old football player faces manslaughter charges in an alcohol-related crash that killed 2 other high school students."

"Recent studies show an increased number of bodybuilders are experiencing irreversible kidney damage from the use of steroids."

"Local college basketball star and 3-other student athletes fight suspension and loss of scholarships stemming from marijuana charges."

"Prescription drug abuse on the rise among former student athletes."

Again, we often assume our children would know better. I am sure many parents of children that have suffered horrific consequences involving drug and alcohol abuse felt the same way at some point. I am sure none of these student athletes expected to have their lives and/or athletic careers end in such senseless tragedies. Do not allow your children to become another preventable, tragic statistics.

AUTOMATED EXTERNAL DEFIBRILLATORS (AED)

The risks of a student athlete going into sudden cardiac arrest is extremely rare. A sudden cardiac arrest is an electrical problem in the heart, which causes the heart to beat in an irregular, inefficient manner. Basically, a person's heart stops pumping blood. Since the blood cannot circulate to the brain, the victim passes out and may suddenly collapse. If this happens, an Automatic External Defibrillator or AED could save that child's life. An AED is a device designed to deliver an electric shock to a victim of sudden cardiac arrest. This device checks a person's heart and delivers an electric shock if it has stopped beating normally. Although training on this device is highly recommended, the device is designed to coach anyone through the process, even without training. The AED provides verbal instructions on how to put the pads on the victim. It will then sense the heart's rhythm and determine the best steps to take. If the AED device determines a shock is necessary it will explain in a calm, clear voice exactly what to do. It actively adapts the instructions to keep you on track. There are intelligent sensors that assess and automatically deliver the right shock, at the right time and it is personalized to every man, woman or child. In essence, this device is extremely user-friendly.

Chances of survival from Sudden Cardiac Arrest decrease 10% for every minute that passes. If defibrillation does not occur within a five to ten minute window, the chances of a victim surviving are almost zero. The

American Heart Association encourages AEDS at all types of fitness centers. Many states have passed AED legislation mandating its placement in school gyms and sporting facilities; however, not every state requires it. (FYI: AEDs are required in all Texas Public schools.) Parents research and inquire about whether or not your school has an AED. If it does not, consider spearheading the movement to get an AED. This device saves lives!

CHAPTER 3

TAKE A KNEE:
Sports injuries, Treatments, and Resources

It is the fourth quarter of the District Championship game and each team can taste sweet victory. The score is tied and the bleachers are filled with fans hungry for a win. Everyone is on their feet with cheers that rock the gym. The ball is in motion. Jay goes up for a clean block and swats the basketball directly into Tyler's hands. Tyler does not hesitate and dribbles the ball full speed down the court hoping for a fast break and an easy layup. Unfortunately, as Tyler goes up for the monster jam— his shot is rejected in mid-air. Consequently, Tyler is slammed to the floor. The impact can be heard by everyone in the building. A player is down. The crowd gasps as Tyler lays motionless. The coaches leap off the bench and the trainers spring into action. The other players all take a knee. An injury can occur in any sport- in any game - to any one of our student athletes -at any level.

Although sports injuries are common, it is likely a student athlete and a parent's worst fear. It is inevitable that if student athletes play sports long enough, they may experience some type of injury. Despite that miracle, 75-yard-return-for-the-winning touchdown that astonished the crowd and had everyone on their feet— your student athlete is still only human, made of flesh and blood. Which means, unfortunately, there is always that looming possibility of an injury.

INSURANCE
Most private health insurance policies will cover injuries your child sustains while playing sports in school. Make sure your personal health insurance is updated. You should also familiarize yourself with urgent care facilities and hospitals that are covered by your insurance plan.

Think about taking advantage of your flexible spending accounts during your insurance enrollment periods. Those co-pays, prescriptions, and other medical expenses you may incur throughout the year can quickly add up. Furthermore, consider tapping into some of those underused coverages your health insurance may provide that you just do not think about. Review your family's health insurance plan carefully to know what coverage is available for your student athletes beyond the usual stuff like coverage for a dietician, nutritionist, chiropractor, counselor, and even a gym membership.

Many may not know that often school districts provide links for insurance for student athletes. Different variations of insurance plans may be provided with cost depending on the coverage offered. For instance, Texas Kids First is an insurance company that currently offers the following selection of plans: "At-School Accident Plan", "24-hour Accident Plan" and even a "Football Accident" Plan. The "At-School Accident Plan" covers a student while participating on school premises or while attending school-sponsored activities and/or athletics away from school premises during the regular school term. You can check your school district's website for information on health insurance alternatives. Parents can determine if these options are a good fit for your household's health insurance needs.

TRAINERS
Parents utilize the trainers. Allow trainers to assess your child's injury and follow their advice. Do not minimize this resource especially in high school and college. Many high school head athletic trainers are experienced, highly educated, and certified. Some may even hold advanced degrees and degrees from accredited professional athletic training programs. These trainers may offer your injured child convenient on site daily services. They are equipped with a variety of useful items such as wraps, gels, crutches, braces etc. Some can even administer physical therapy as needed. Usually, the higher the level your student athlete competes, the more resources are available for the

trainers. Be sure to inquire about these free resources available for your child.

SPORTS MEDICINE DOCTORS

If your child suffers a serious injury such as a broken bone or a torn ligament, consider finding a sports medicine doctor. Sports medicine doctors are usually well-versed with sports injuries. Also, they are usually on the cutting edge of technology and research with different types of sports injuries. A sports medicine specialist will bring a higher level of expertise and may be able to offer more options for treatment. If surgery is ever recommended by any doctor, be sure to get a second and even third opinion before you make a final decision.

SEXUAL PREDATORS

Also, be aware if student athletes are injured they may spend more one-on-one time with trainers and medical professionals. Remember while they are recovering they may be in a vulnerable state. Parents we must make sure student athletes are NOT AFRAID to tell a parent about any concerns about inappropriate behavior of a trainer, a coach, or a medical professional. If something doesn't feel right to them, they should feel comfortable enough to say something. It's ALWAYS better to err on the side of caution. In recent years, we have seen disturbing things in the news involving trainers and sports doctors taking advantage of student athletes' vulnerability, trust, and sheer desire to just get back in the game. Parents you should be mindful and stay involved and aware. Make an effort to meet and get to know the trainers, therapists, and doctors especially if your child has sustained an injury that requires routine treatment with a trainer or medical professional.

CONCUSSIONS

Concussions have in recent years gained a lot of attention especially involving the game of football. Understand concussions can happen in any sport. Although some concussion symptoms may appear within minutes of the injury, some symptoms may take several hours to occur.

If student athletes experience unconsciousness during a sports-related impact, they should be examined for a concussion or a spine injury. Parents keep in mind some symptoms of concussions are: headaches, loss of consciousness, feeling in a "fog," equilibrium off, nausea/vomiting, memory loss, mood changes, enlarged pupils, double or blurred vision, speech impairment, excessive drowsiness, and difficulty falling asleep.

If your student athlete experiences a concussion, your child should NEVER just continue to play through the game or practice. Instead your child should be allowed to rest until symptoms subside. This allows the brain to recover. Rest involves allowing time to sleep or take frequent naps. Minimizing distractions such as television, internet, reading, or phone use is important. The athlete should avoid pain relievers like aspirin or other anti-inflammatory medications as this may increase the risk of bleeding in the brain. Never leave your child experiencing symptoms alone. Monitor symptoms closely and if they worsen, the athlete may need to be evaluated in the emergency room to determine if there is a more serious brain injury. A person can recover from a concussion in as little as 24 hours, but symptoms can persist for up to three weeks.

CHRONIC TRAUMATIC ENCEPHALOPATHY (CTE)
This is a degenerative brain condition and is associated with concussions and/or repeated blows to the head over a period of years. CTE is caused by a buildup of an abnormal protein called tau that kills brain cells. The protein seems to affect areas of the brain that control memory, emotions, and other critical brain functions. Consequently, the symptoms of CTE include mood disorders, cognitive difficulties, impulsiveness, headaches, memory loss, and even dementia. Symptoms can surface gradually or appear suddenly. Some research concludes that chances of developing CTE and the severity of its condition can be attributed to several factors. Children who play contact sports during their most critical years of brain development are believed to be more susceptible to have neurological

impairments and CTE later in life. In addition, the higher the level of play and the greater the length of time someone plays contact sports seems to increase the chances of having CTE and increases its severity. You can reference a popular website CTEsociety.org for more information).

Keep in mind CTE and its correlation to contact sports is still a very highly debated issue. Research is still being conducted and evidence gathered. Some have questioned whether the studies and research done are objective and/or even accurate. There is a lot of uncertainty that looms around the actual diagnosis as people can only be diagnosed with 100% accuracy after death. This is when a person's brain tissue can be analyzed. A lot of the current research relies on interviews with former players at different levels regarding symptoms and experiences. Parents, you should be aware and knowledgeable of the possible risk and make your own informed decisions concerning contact sports and your children.

EMOTIONAL WELLNESS

If your student athlete is injured, your child must emotionally process the medical information about the injury while processing the actual pain, discomfort, and physical limitations caused by the injury. You may notice your child may experience irritation, sadness, isolation, lack of motivation, frustration, anger, changes in appetite, changes in sleep patterns etc. More than likely, your child will work through all of this and make a full recovery physically and emotionally. However, sometimes when a student has an injury it can trigger deeper psychological issues. Remember our students are young and are still developing. Some student athletes place so much emphasis on being an athlete, they have difficulty realizing there is so much more to their identity and self-worth than the sport they play. Consequently, if an injury is serious and threatens to affect their ability to play the sport they love and have invested so much—they may experience anxiety, depression, eating disorders and/or even substance abuse. There is no predictable sequence or reaction in which a student may respond to an injury. For this reason, parents be cautious and monitor your children's emotional wellness throughout their recovery. Seek counseling if you feel it's needed. We will discuss emotional wellness more in Chapter 4.

TRADITIONAL AND NON-TRADITIONAL TREATMENTS

R-I-C-E. If your student athlete has ever experienced a sprain or strain, you may already know RICE is more than just one of the most popular grain food products in the world. R-I-C-E is an acronym that refers to a commonly recommended treatment for sprains and strains within 24-72 hours after an injury. (A strain is a stretch or tear in a muscle or tendon; whereas, a sprain is a stretch or tear in a ligament). The acronym R-I-C-E stands for rest, ice, compression, and elevation. You can reduce swelling, ease pain, and speed up healing using this R-I-C-E method.

Physical Therapy. Ever hear a person complain about an old sports injury that still gives them problems years later? Ever heard of a student athlete that has experienced a recurrent injury (i.e, a sprained ankle, knee injury) over and over? Perhaps, physical therapy could have improved those outcomes.

A physical therapist can determine the extent of an injury and use techniques to minimize further damage; speed up the recovery and healing process; strengthen and stretch muscles; minimize swelling and pain; and restore a normal range of motion. The length of physical therapy treatment may depend on the type of injury and its severity. For example, the severity of a strain and sprain are categorized as first degree, second degree and third degree- with third degree being the most severe. A physical therapist can assess the injury and customize a program for an injured athlete to get the best recovery results possible.

Why opt for physical therapy? Physical therapy improves the chance of collagen fibers being aligned back to their natural state around an injured area. Collagen is a structural protein and is the most abundant protein in the human body. Collagen can be thought of as a building block that supports many tissues and structures throughout our body parts i.e., muscles, tendons, ligaments and bones. When an area of the body is injured, scar tissue forms after an injury to normal collagen tissue. This is all part of the normal healing process. Problems arise when collagen cells do not align correctly during the recovery process. When this occurs, it may cause adhesions and formations that will cause an injured area to lose its flexibility, structure, and range of motion. Stretching scar tissue, helps to align collagen fibers properly so that they return to normal. The process is called remodeling. When collagen fibers are properly realigned, the injured area is able to regain it flexibility, stability, and range of motion. Proper alignment of collagen fibers also reduces the chance of subsequent injury.

A therapist may use various methods such as exercises, taping, electrical stimulation, and massage techniques to achieve optimum recovery results. These practices can help flush out swelling in joints; loosen scar tissue and help collagen fibers align properly; and increase blood flow to heal the damaged area. For these reasons and more, I implore every parent of an injured student athlete to consult with your doctor and consider physical therapy options if recommended.

Ice baths or cold-water immersion (CWI) therapy. This is a form of therapy your student athlete might want to try to help soothe sore muscles after a serious work out or a game. The idea is to immerse the body in freezing cold water to reduce the body temperature, blood flow, and inflammation in tissues of the muscles. When the whole body or parts of the body are immersed in a bathtub or even a bucket of frigid ice water for a limited duration, this constricts blood vessels, flushes waste products, and reduces swelling in tissue breakdown. As the tissue warms, the increased blood flow speeds circulation, which aids in the healing process.

Baths. A warm bath is the original hydrotherapy water treatment. Heat therapy promotes blood flow, helps muscles relax, loosens stiff joints and it can be relaxing for the mind. Some key things to remember while taking warm baths:

- Make sure water is not too hot.
- Keep a cool head while soaking in warm water. Keep a cool towel on your forehead or around your neck.
- Stay hydrated. Drink cool water while soaking.
- Try light stretching exercises while immersed in the bathtub.
- Add Epsom salt in your bathwater.

Medications. Medical professionals may sometimes prescribe medication to your children for pain, inflammation, and sickness. Parents, you should always carefully monitor your children's usage of any medication prescribed by a doctor and even over the counter (OTC) medications. Be sure the medication is taken in the right dosage and at the appropriate times. Pay attention to possible reactions with other medications. Read whether or not medication should be taken with or without food. Remind your children, medicines are still drugs and should be handled responsibly.

Yoga. Practicing yoga on a regular basis improves the health of your bones while strengthening your spine. Furthermore, yoga stretches and strengthens muscles, tendons, and ligaments. This makes them less susceptible to strain and breakdown. Yoga poses can increase blood circulation, which can bring healing nutrients to injured tissues.

Essential oils. The history of essential oils can be traced back to Ancient Egypt. It has been an age-long belief that there are healing properties in essential oils. There are hundreds of phytochemicals (plant based chemicals) within each drop of an essential oil. It is believed each of these phytochemicals work differently to provide various benefits to the body. Not all essential oils are created equal. When choosing an essential oil, you must select brands that properly extract their oil product, have an effective distillation process, and regularly batch test their oil products to ensure quality is preserved. Check the ingredients to ensure the oil is in its purest state possible. The ingredients should not include chemical additives or unnecessary fillers. Per Dr. Tammye Turner, "Essential oils that are more potent are more effective." Some reputable brands for essential oils include the following: Young Living, Doterra, Mountain Rose, and Aura Cacia.

There are many different essential oils and some can be used for multiple purposes. You can experiment and will likely find your favorites. Some of the best oils to use for sickness include: wintergreen, peppermint, eucalyptus, lemon oil, cinnamon, rosemary, frankincense, and ginger. Some popular oils that are used to sooth muscles and relax the body include: lavender, eucalyptus, and chamomile. Here are few popular ways to use essential oils:

1) Rub essential oils on the soles of your feet. Essential oils are better able to be absorbed into the body through the soles of the feet because the soles of your feet do NOT have sebaceous glands. (Sebaceous glands secrete sebum which act as barriers for the skin.)

2) Put essential oils into a diffuser. Diffusers can break down essential oils into microparticles. This allows the essential oils to be dispersed as a mist mixed with steam into the air and breathed into the body.

3) Apply a few drops of essential oils into the bath water. The warmth of the bath water can help your children's skin to better absorb the therapeutic properties of essential oils while the fragrance is inhaled simultaneously.

4) Apply essential oils directly to the skin using carrier oils with a cotton ball. When applying directly to the skin, carrier oils (i.e., coconut oil or jojoba oil) should be used to help essential oils absorb into the skin more easily.

Chakras. The Chakra system originated in India many years ago. It is believed the body is a self-healing mechanism and has spiritual portals. Chakras are believed to be energy centers within the human body that help to regulate all of the body's processes, from organ functions to the immune system and emotions. They include energies linked to our thoughts, creativity, determination, compassion, intuitiveness, etc. It is believed that there are seven chakras positioned throughout our body from the base of our spine to the crown of our head. Each chakra has its own vibrational frequency that is depicted through a specific chakra color, and governs specific functions that can allow us to operate at our optimal and feel our best.

These are the names, colors, and anatomical location of seven chakras in the body:

The Base/Root Chakra	Red	Base of spine of spine
The Sacral Chakra	Orange	Below navel, lower abdomen
The Solar Plexus Chakra	Yellow	Above navel, stomach area
The Heart Chakra	Green	Center of chest
The Throat Chakra	Blue	Throat region
The Third Eye Chakra	Indigo	Forehead in between the eyes
The Crown Chakra	Violet	Top of head

There are several exercises, poses, breathing techniques, and meditation methods that are recommended to open and balance the chakra channels. It is believed when all of the body's chakras are open and balanced, it will allow energy to flow freely within our body and achieve optimal wellness. (A good read on this subject is The Solar Body: The Secret to Natural Healing by Ilchi Lee.)

Cryotherapy. Cryotherapy is an innovative, holistic, wellness experience that enables the human body to recover and rejuvenate itself naturally. It may look like a futuristic machine you are entering into with smoke all around; however, the benefits experienced are real for many athletes. Cryotherapy exposes the body to extremely low temperatures and can treat tissue damage. It helps reduce inflammation and increases cell rejuvenation.. The body's exposure to extremely cold temperatures (-110 degrees Celsius) stimulates thermoreceptors in the skin and activates a central nervous system (CNS) response. Your blood circulation will improve the production of serotonin and endorphins and natural anti-inflammatories that will be set into motion. Toxins are immediately disposed of by the stronger flow of oxygen and nutrient-rich blood. The body scans itself for poorly functioning parts and sets recovery processes into motion. Cryotherapy is a unique experience that many athletes have started to include as part of their routine. The cost per session are reasonable but the average sessions are usually only about 2-3 minutes. Check your local listings for facilities that offer cryotherapy in your area.

Transcutaneous Electrical Nerve Stimulation (TENS Unit). A TENS unit is a small, battery operated device that transmits an electric signal through self-adhesive pads that are placed on areas of the body that have pain. A TENS unit has various modes and settings (i.e., rub and knead) that can be adjusted to your preference. It's like having your own personal masseuse with a little bit of zap.

There are different theories about how TENS units actual reduce or stop pain. One theory suggests the TENS unit sends an electric signal that passes through the skin to nerve fibers and stops pain signals before they reach the brain. Since the signals do not reach the brain —then no pain is felt. The other theory is a TENS unit increases the body's production of endorphins, which is a natural painkiller. Both theories agree, TENS units are safe and very effective for pain management.

Personal TENS units are reasonably priced and can be purchased at many local corner pharmacy stores. **As with any device, be sure to read and follow all instructions carefully.** The device itself can be shared with multiple family members; however, you should not share sets of pads. You should purchase separate sets of pads for each individual and be sure to replace pads as needed. A TENS unit is a good investment for any household that has a student athlete.

Please note: Doctors should ALWAYS be consulted before experimenting with any of the aforementioned treatment options, especially if your child has any known prior medical conditions

CHAPTER 4

THE BODY ACHIEVES WHAT THE MIND BELIEVES:
Emotional Wellness and Mental Toughness

Parents you must remember the competitive nature of a student athlete often does not come with an "off switch." Students are still developing coping skills and parents must always keep this in mind. Their schedules get super hectic and finding a balance for their academic, physical, and social demands may sometimes prove to be quite the challenge. There are many documented cases of overachieving student athletes suffering from mental health issues (i.e., anxiety, depression, addictions, etc.) caused by their inability to keep different aspects of their lives in perspective. Oftentimes, their identities may be overshadowed by playing sports. As the stakes get higher and the pressure to perform becomes greater and greater- personal, academic, and social demands can easily become overwhelming. Children must be taught skills to keep an emotional balance to successfully maneuver through this maze. Achieving and maintaining emotional balance is an ongoing journey that needs to start as early as possible with your student athlete.

MENTAL TOUGHNESS
What exactly is mental toughness? There are so many descriptions associated with "mental toughness" as it relates to sports. Some describe mental toughness as the ability to play with confidence and be laser focused-no matter what happens in the game. Others may describe mental toughness as the ability to play with an elevated IQ; whereas, you simply outthink your opponents and you are able to maximize all of your strengths and take advantage of their weaknesses. Still others may say it is the relentless belief and pursuit of a win. Digging deep and pulling out all the stops.

Some of "The Greats" have eloquently commented on this very subject:

"Concentration and mental toughness are the margins of victory." - Bill Russell

"These young guys are playing checkers. I'm out there playing chess."-Kobe Bryant

"The thing about the game at this level is that there is very little difference in physical skills between players; the real difference between them is upstairs. It is what's in your head that makes the difference."-Cletis "Clete" Boyer

Spectators have described mentally tough players as being "locked in", "in-the- zone", "flow ready" or playing in "beast mode." Whatever you call it, it is extremely impressive and exciting for sports fans to watch. It is also the level of play in which every player should aspire to reach.

So how do we equip our student athletes to become mentally tough and achieve emotional balance? Teach them to train their minds like they do their bodies. The following are some practices that may assist in this training process.

Prayer. Prayer involves making a spiritual connection and is an intimate form of communication (talking and listening) with a higher being. When people pray they may express gratitude and/or just humbly make requests for guidance with an issue. There is a basic premise that there is no circumstance that can not be remedied. This is part of what makes prayer so comforting and so powerful. For Christians scripture says, "We can do all things through Christ that strengthens us." (Philippians 4:13). Establishing a spiritual foundation and learning to pray effectively is a life changing experience that student athletes can incorporate in sports and in all aspects of their lives.

Meditation. Some of the greatest athletes of all times have tapped into the power of mediation to improve their focus, reduce stress, and gain a competitive edge. Meditation and mindfulness have been practiced by many professional athletes, teams, coaches and more. You know their names - Kobe Bryant, Phil Jackson, the Colts are just a few sports figures and sports teams that have practiced meditation to yield positive results.

Some forms of meditation include visualization, deep breathing exercises, stillness and silence, and affirmations. Visualization is the practice of mentally envisioning yourself executing a goal. When children can close their eyes and picture the step-by-step actions to reach a goal, that particular goal becomes more real and attainable. Also, deep breathing exercises can calm nerves and teach them to selectively focus. Stillness and silence can help children stay centered.

Affirmations. Affirmations are considered a form of meditation. Affirmations are repeated positive statements designed to yield a desired outcome. It is believed the Reticular Activating System (RAS) is part of our brain that allow words that are repeated over a period of time to become part of our identity. Affirmations are a spiritual concept as well as a Biblical principle. Positive affirmations can be a powerful mental tool for your student athlete.

Perhaps one of the best examples is the late Great Muhammad Ali. Ali's infamous affirmation, "I Am The Greatest," ultimately defined his destiny. Muhammad Ali once so eloquently stated, "It's the repetition of affirmations that lead to belief. And once that belief becomes a deep conviction, things begin to happen."

Sports fans get it too. Game crowds lock into chants for their team. One popular affirmation that sports fans have used is "I believe that we will win!" Affirmations can stir up all kinds of positive energy and help players tap into their greatness.

Encourage your children to practice using positive self affirmations. It does not have to be anything dramatic but it should be consistent and personal. "I am strong." "I am fast." "I will be a beast on defense." Affirmations should be repeated often. Your child can even post affirmations in their locker, on their bathroom mirror, or even as a screensaver on their electronic devices. Whatever it takes to get it into their psyche.

Parents we should also practice using positive affirmations. Whoever said, "Sticks and stones may break my bones but words can never hurt me"-they lied. There is power in words! The right words can encourage and inspire and build up a child. The wrong words, can break spirits and cast doubt! As parents, if we can practice reinforcing positive affirmations with our children, it can be a game changer in building their confidence in sports and in life.

EMOTIONAL INTELLIGENCE

Emotional intelligence is a person's ability to recognize emotions, understand the powerful effects of emotions, and actually use that information to guide their thinking and behavior. Developing and practicing emotional intelligence will help children better understand themselves and others. This will help them make more insightful choices. Furthermore, having an elevated Emotional Intelligence IQ will help a child become more emotionally balanced and mentally tough.

So how emotionally intelligent is your child? How would your child react if he/she gets "benched"? What would happen if a referee makes a bad call against your child that cost the game? How would your child respond to trash talking and/or a flagrant foul? When those dramatic circumstances arise in a game, maybe your child will respond exactly how you think but maybe not.

Student athletes should all make a conscious effort to increase their emotional intelligence to be equipped to handle heightened situations as it relates to sports and life. Here are some pointers to increase your children's emotional intelligence IQ:

1) Self-Reflect. Encourage your children to reflect upon their own emotions. If children are mindful of how they typically react emotionally, it can help them build self-control over their emotions and make improvements.

2) Ask others for perspective. Your children should be comfortable asking for an outside trusted opinion. Sometimes we may perceive ourselves differently than others perceive us. Knowledge of how others perceive our actions may provide critical needed insight for your child.

3) Be observant. Children should learn to develop an awareness of body language, tones, and other nonverbal signals from others. In doing so, children will learn how to better process the reactions of others and adjust their own reactions accordingly.

4) Pause. Our children must learn to take a moment to stop and think before speaking or acting- especially when emotions are running high. This may save a lot of hardships, hurt feelings, and irrevocable consequences.

5) Think about the "whys." Everything may not always be what it seems. We should encourage our children to be understanding, empathetic, and compassionate towards others by trying to see the situation through the other person's eyes.

6) Don't be defensive. Our children should recognize that they can learn more if they are open to constructive criticism. Being defensive can hinder growth.

The more children use the aforementioned strategies and concepts, the more emotionally intelligent they will become. Emotional intelligence builds leaders on and off the court.

SOCIAL INTERACTION
Social interactions play a very influential role in the development of your child's nature and ideals of people. It can also serve as a stress reliever and an emotional outlet.

Parents should encourage your children to socialize in person. This is quickly becoming a lost art thanks to the popularity of social media and busy schedules. A hug, a handshake, or a pat on the back can 't be done through social media and that is the reason social media should not be a complete substitute for face-to-face contact. Socializing in person can include casual routines like having dinner with the family, hanging out with friends or teammates, and/or participating in church or community group activities. These are all very healthy habits for student athletes to incorporate into their schedules. Making time for these things can provide a loving, fun, and supportive environment for your children and help them keep and maintain a balance.

Fortunately and unfortunately, social media is a part of our children's world. Some uses of social media are great. You can post videos from the games and send and receive "shout outs." However, some aspects of social media are negative and filled with "hatorade." Even though children cannot prevent others from posting negative comments or giving unsolicited advice, remind them they can control what they choose to read and how they react. Consider limiting your child's activity on social media so they will learn to unplug from "the twenty-four-seven-social-media machine" and be present in the moment.

SLEEP

Sleep can make the world look very different from an emotional standpoint and make you feel mentally tougher. Ever been so upset about something, but after a good night's sleep the issue does not seem as big of an issue anymore? People usually have a sharper, clearer mind when they get good sleep. Parents, help instill good sleep habits into your children early. Turn off electronic devices and TVs and set a time for your children to sleep. Also, make sure they sleep in a comfortable bed as opposed to a couch or chair. Ensure your child gets the proper quantity and quality sleep.

MUSIC

Music and sports have had a long standing relationship with athletes. Studies show music can help athletes improve their mood, reduce feelings of fatigue, and increase their tolerance of pain. Athletes who tap into the right music find it easier to block out feelings of panic and worry and redirect their focus to feelings of confidence and success. Parents, if your children are not already incorporating music into their workouts or pre-game prep rituals —try it. Let them get a workout playlist together as well as a pregame playlist to help improve their athletic performance. Music motivates!

CHAPTER 5
The "Hippocrates Effect"
Healthy Food Choices

"Let food be thy medicine and medicine be thy food."-Hippocrates

Hippocrates summed up what every student athlete should already know— food choices are important to your body. Everything we eat has an effect on our body. Like medicine, food choices can help or hinder the body's performance. When we teach our children the different components of a healthy diet, we equip them to make better food choices and have a healthier diet. The "Hippocrates Effect" can help propel your children's athletic performance. Parents, remind your children their performance in those games will be in part a reflection of their food choices.

COMPONENTS OF A HEALTHY DIET
Carbohydrates. For almost every sport, carbs are going to be an important part of what athletes consume. Carbohydrates provide energy. The key for student athletes is choosing good quality foods with carbs. Even though many children can appreciate a good Snickers bar, which is actually loaded with carbs, a candy bar may not be a good choice for children before a two-hour practice. They might get a quick burst of energy, but it will not last long. The problem is carbohydrates from candy bars come from processed sugars and have very little fiber. The body dumps sugar into the bloodstream and that kick of energy will not last long. In other words, the body will crash.

There are better food choices to achieve and maintain elevated energy from carbohydrates. If your children choose carbohydrates with fiber, their bodies will not just dump the sugar into their bloodstream. The fiber will slow down the absorption by the body, releasing the sugar into the bloodstream, a little at a time. This will give your children energy for a longer period. Whole grain cereals, whole grain breads, fresh fruits, vegetables, and dairy products (i.e., yogurt, milk, and cheese) are all better choices. The quest should be to choose carbohydrates your children find tasty and can get the same kick of energy that will last longer.

Fiber. Ever remember being asked poop-related questions when you were a child and had a stomach ache? When was the last time you pooped? Did you poop a little or a lot? Was it loose or did you have to strain? I remember thinking back then, "Is all that information really necessary?" Now I understand these are valid questions, and I find myself asking the same questions as a parent with my children when they complain of stomach aches.

Having the right amount of fiber plays a vital role in the digestive health for our children's bodies. Fiber helps regulate the body's use of sugars. Furthermore, fiber aids in the removal of waste from our bodies. As fiber passes through the stomach and intestines, it absorbs water and helps bulk up our stools.

There are two forms of fiber, soluble and insoluble. Soluble fibers dissolve in water and may help your body absorb vital nutrients from food. Insoluble fibers stay in its fibrous form and helps food pass through the digestive system and adds bulk. Understanding the role that fiber plays in energy and digestion can help our children reach optimal levels of performance and avoid or at least minimize those dreaded stomach issues.

Oftentimes, our children are not getting enough fiber. Fiber can be found in the following: fruits (pears, oranges, apples); vegetables (the darker the color the higher the fiber content); beans; chia seeds; and popcorn.

Too much fiber can cause your student athlete to experience bloating, gas, cramping, and constipation. Relief can be found by increasing liquids. Changes of fiber intake should be gradual to allow your body time to adjust. The recommended fiber intake is as follows per kidshealth.org:

Age	Grams of fiber/daily
Toddlers (1-3 years old)	14 grams
Boys and Girls (4-8 years old)	17-20 grams
Girls (9-13)	22 grams
Girls (14-18)	25 grams
Boys (9-13)	25 grams
Boys (14-18)	31 grams

Unsaturated Fats. The word "fat" usually has a negative connotation associated with it; however, healthy fats have many benefits for your children's bodies. Healthy fats provide energy, develop muscles, regulate temperature, and help the absorption of vitamins.

Fats, like carbohydrates, are sources of energy. Unlike carbohydrates, energy from fat is not so easy for the body to access. Carbs go directly into the student athletes' bloodstream giving instant energy. To release the energy from fats, it must first be broken down into fatty acids and other components before it can be used by the muscles. Fats also help us absorb certain vitamins, specifically vitamins A, D, E, and K. Consider meat, dairy, soybean, and nut oils when preparing foods.

Protein. There is a pretty good chance that when you think of an athlete's diet, the very first thing to come to mind is protein--and for good reason. Your children's bodies need protein. Proteins are the building blocks of body tissue and provide a fuel source. Good sources of proteins include, fish (like salmon, mackerel and trout), poultry, and beef. For non meat eaters eggs, any kind of beans, lentils, tofu, and peanut butter are all excellent sources of protein.

Minerals. We have heard our body needs vitamins and minerals, but what exactly are minerals? What do they do? Our bodies are made of many cells that require essential nutrients to grow, develop, and thrive. Minerals are essential nutrients the human body needs but cannot produce on its own. There are two kinds of minerals-macro minerals and trace minerals.

Macro minerals.
Calcium. Calcium is needed to build strong bones and teeth. Calcium also plays a role in nerve transmissions, muscle function, and hormone secretion. Good sources of calcium include dairy products like yogurt, milk, and vegetables (i.e., cabbage, kale, and broccoli).

Potassium. Potassium controls the electrical activity of your heart and muscle contractions. Your body also uses potassium to build proteins, break down and use carbohydrates, maintain the pH balance of the blood and support normal growth. Foods that contain a good source of potassium include bananas, avocados, tomatoes, fish, beef, and chicken.

Magnesium. Magnesium supports muscle and nerve function, keeps your heart beating regularly, builds strong bones, and boosts immunity. Beans, nuts, whole grains and green vegetables serve as good sources of magnesium.

Phosphorus. Phosphorus repairs cells and tissue and helps with growth. Your children can get this mineral from nuts, poultry, meat, fish, eggs and beans.

Sodium. Sodium is needed to stimulate nerve and muscle function; maintain the correct balance of fluid in the cells; and support the absorption of other nutrients including chloride, amino acids, and glucose. Too much sodium can stiffen blood vessels and hold excess fluid in the body which creates an added burden on the heart. This can cause high blood pressure.

Chloride. Chloride is usually consumed as a salt compound and is better known as table salt. It balances the fluids in your body and plays an essential role in the production of digestive juices in the stomach.

Trace minerals.
Our body only needs a very small amount of trace minerals. Like macro minerals, trace minerals also support important bodily functions.

Iron produces hemoglobin and myoglobin- proteins that carry oxygen in your body. Iodine is needed for the production of thyroid hormones that regulate nearly every cell in the body. Manganese regulates blood sugar, enhances the absorption of calcium, and plays a role in the production of connective tissues and bones. Chromium enhances the action of insulin, making it important in regulating blood sugar. Fluoride keeps your teeth strong and healthy. Copper, selenium, molybdenum and zinc produce enzymes important in various reactions throughout the body.

If you suspect your child may have a mineral deficiency, discuss with your child's doctor. They can ask more probing questions regarding symptoms and can order blood work for your child if they deem it necessary.

Water. The human body is comprised of at least 60% water and water has many critical functions. Water helps improve digestion; carries nutrients and oxygen to our cells; prevents constipation; flushes bacteria from our bladders; regulates blood pressure and body temperature; cushions joints; protects organs; and helps maintain electrolyte balance. In essence, **water does the body good**.

Medical experts may vary in their opinions as to how much water your children should drink daily. Some experts say children should consume a minimum of at least half their body weight in ounces of water. For instance, if your child weighs 100 lbs he/she should drink at least 50 ounces of water daily. Other experts advise that children should drink when they are thirsty. They feel this should be sufficient because they get water from other sources (i.e., foods and other beverages). Still other experts advise that children should drink 6-8 cups daily. Although opinions may vary about the recommended amount of daily water consumption for children, most all experts agree they should increase their water intake when engaging in vigorous exercise or if the weather is hot. In these cases, children sweat more and will lose fluids at a faster rate.

It is critical that your student athletes understand the importance of staying hydrated. Dehydration is a condition caused by excessive loss of water from the body. Not having enough fluids coming into the body can disrupt balance and compromise your children's ability to regulate their temperature and function properly. Symptoms of dehydration include: headaches, fainting or feeling faint, dizziness, dry skin, inability to urinate, dark urine, and dry mouth. If your child experiences any of these symptoms, insist they drink more water (small sips) or seek medical attention if symptoms are more severe.

NUTRITIONAL SUPPLEMENTS

Vitamins. If your children eat healthy well-balanced meals with a variety of meats, seafood, vegetables, fruits, whole grains and oats—there is a pretty good chance your children are getting most of the vitamins they need. Getting vitamins from a well-balanced healthy diet is definitely the preferred method for your children to receive nutrients for their bodies. This increases the likelihood the nutrients are being absorbed and used by the body. Food not only supplies vitamins and minerals but also gives us fiber and a host of other health compounds that interact with each other in ways vitamin supplements can not. Nevertheless, if your child's best dietary efforts fall short or they are picky eaters, you may want to consider vitamin supplements.

Juicing. Juicing is the process of extracting juice from fresh fruits or vegetables. You will need to invest in a juicer not just a blender.

Theoretically, the better the quality of the juicer the more efficient the extraction process will be. Vegetable juicing is fine, but try to limit fruit juicing. Without the fiber from the fruit, the juice has a high concentration of sugar. It also requires far more of the fruit to create a sufficient amount of juice, so you consume more of the concentrated sugar. When juicing you should use organic ingredients to avoid pesticides.

Smoothies. Smoothies blend various foods together. Most include a base like yogurt, almond milk, etc. There are plenty of good healthy smoothie recipes out there. Help your student athletes find a combination that appeals to their taste buds. Make sure it includes essential greenery, fiber and very limited sugar. Again, remember to use organic ingredients to avoid pesticides.

Things to Remember. Minimize sugar and sugary drinks, processed foods, artificial sweeteners, energy drinks, candy, and fast food. Use garlic and onions generously to help detoxify the body. Drink lots of water. Remember organic ingredients are healthier when preparing smoothies or juicing as they limit exposure to pesticides.

WEIGHT CHANGES

I know this topic is a very touchy subject but like it or not, it may be a real scenario for some student athletes. What if the coach suggests your child needs to "beef up" or either drop a few pounds for a particular sport or to play a certain position? Parents, be aware of weight-related messages your children may be receiving from coaches, peers, and the world. It is worth having a real conversation about healthy weight changes and a positive body image with your student athletes. After all, their bodies are constantly on display as athletes; consequently, they may be subject to more criticism and scrutiny than the average person.

Sometimes student athletes that are trying to improve their sports performance consider weight changes. Weight changes should never be viewed lightly. Student athletes should understand a healthy weight range for their frame should always be the ultimate goal. Student athletes should strive to be the healthiest they can be and should never be influenced otherwise. If someone suggests they gain or lose weight outside of a healthy weight range for their frame, it should never be an option. Remind them the perfect weight is not a set number for everyone and one size does not fit all. Everyone burns calories at a different rate for different reasons. Student athletes must devise an individual plan of action, which should include consultation with a doctor, a healthy diet, and exercise.

There are some other critical things parents and student athletes should keep in mind regarding weight changes. One being, it is often more beneficial to monitor athletic performance (i.e., speed, strength, agility) rather than weight. Secondly, your child should understand weight and body mass index (BMI) are not good indicators of body fat and lean muscle. Body composition measurements, which determine the percentage of body fat and lean tissue, should also be considered. Thirdly, if a child is under twelve years of age, losing weight can potentially affect normal growth and development. Oftentimes, doctors recommend overweight younger children focus on maintaining their weight and just allow their bodies to grow into it rather than trying to lose weight. On the flip side, parents should also understand efforts to gain weight before puberty may NOT necessarily lead to increased muscle but may instead lead to increased fat.

If your child is older and determined to gain weight, within a healthy weight range for their body frame, they should adjust their diet and choice of exercise. They can add more protein, carbs, fat, and dairy while limiting sugar. Your child should never practice overindulgence to gain weight but rather consider increasing the number of healthy meals they eat throughout the day. As far as exercise, lifting weights or exercises using their own body weight (i.e., push ups) can be helpful in bulking up your student athlete.

When it comes to weight loss, the same concept applies. They should adjust their diet and their workouts accordingly. Remember when weight comes off gradually it will last longer and these are the healthiest changes for the body. Student athletes hoping to drop a few pounds within a healthy weight range for their body frame may opt to adjust calorie intake and try to incorporate more cardio. Again, parents monitor your children to make sure your children are not obsessing over weight loss.

All things considered, weight changes are an extremely sensitive subject because we do not ever want our children grappling with negative body images. If a child is determined to shed a few pounds or gain weight, parents and doctors should be involved in the process to ensure the child remains realistic with expectations and takes the healthiest approach possible.

PLANNING MEALS AND SNACKS

It's not realistic to expect your children will have an absolutely perfect diet. As kids get older, they have more autonomy over what they eat. They can buy their own snacks, sodas, chips, candy and more without our knowledge- and they do! As parents, our energy is probably better spent providing high quality options at home and educating children about nutrition at an early age so that their food choices are as healthy as possible. Here are some helpful hints:

- Grocery shop with healthy components of a diet in mind. Protein for strength, fiber for digestive health, and carbs for energy, etc.
- Plan menus for the week. If you plan, it is easier to stick to your health goals.
- Find healthy recipes. You can find recipes online, cookbooks, cooking shows, etc. You can experiment and get a few staple meals, "go to recipes", then you can mix and match others.

- Cook and freeze meals for later if you recognize some days will be more hectic than others. This will help you avoid or limit fast food alternatives as meal choices.
- Teach your children to cook and prepare healthy meals.
- Pack healthy snacks for your children to ensure healthy snacks are readily available to them throughout the day. Making healthy snack choices convenient for your student athlete can influence them to stay on track.
- Teach children to make healthy food choices when they dine out. Look for healthy food options on menus at their favorite restaurants.

Keep in mind, learning how good food choices directly affect your body's performance will give your children a solid foundation for maintaining a healthy lifestyle. The benefits of learning to eat healthy will be reaped throughout their lifetime, long after their journey as a student athlete is over.

HALF-TIME SPOTLIGHTS

HALF-TIME SPOTLIGHTS

HALF-TIME CONVERSATIONS WITH COACHES

What have you observed as being some of the most difficult challenges student athletes encounter adjusting from playing high school to college sports?

I believe the adjustment that most student athletes face is actually the freedom of movement and managing their own schedule of priorities. In almost every instance, there is a transitional time where the athlete will also need to adjust their game. The level of talent they are facing is greater and the number of competitions played in college as opposed to high school is a lot more. I have found that most students make those adjustments to their game over time naturally but many will struggle most with time management and academics.

-Fred Washington, Former Athletic Director at Prairie View A&M University

What advice would you give parents of student athletes trying to put in some extra work training?

"Perfect Practice Makes Perfect Performance." The proper effort and time must be put forward to achieve your goals. Training involves more than going to practice and running until you throw up or pass out. You have to strategically engage in exercises and drills that maximize your results and performance. Be committed. Be persistent. Be consistent."

-Coach D. King, Drills=Skills

HALF-TIME CONVERSATIONS WITH COACHES

How do you deal with multiple sport athletes? Do you feel they eventually need to make a choice?
"I encourage multiple sports but I also encourage breaks. It is hard to do it all but I tell players that if you are doing it all, it will be hard for you to become great at one sport. Those who do one sport are growing and focused on one thing all the time. When you play multiple sports, you have to share your time."
M. Mcgregor, High School Coach

What advice would you give a parent of a student athlete, when a student athlete is injured?
"When your athlete is injured, let them heal. They only get one body and they need to take care of it."
M. Mcgregor, HS Coach

What are some things about coaching that parents and their children do not understand that you wish they did? "It's not always about winning or losing, winning is not everything but rather the process of learning how to deal with both wins and losses. It takes discipline to persevere and succeed as a team."
-A. Gonzalez, HS Coach

What are some characteristics you believe are mandatory for student athletes to possess to be good competitors? "Tenacity, aggressiveness, the ability to endure physical challenges, and a real desire to be competitive."**-Coach Johnnie Means, Harris County Aquatics Commissioner**

HALF-TIME CONVERSATIONS WITH COACHES

What are the benefits of playing AAU basketball?
Older and younger students can benefit from playing AAU basketball. Younger athletes will learn the fundamentals of the game and get a solid foundation. As students get older, playing AAU sports becomes an opportunity to play in front of college coaches to earn scholarships and a college education.

Playing AAU basketball teaches all student athletes how to earn the coach's trust, earn more playing time, and develop a good work ethic. Furthermore, AAU teaches players how to be a part of a team. Being a great teammate is paramount because this shows that a player cares about the success and accomplishments of others too. All great players must learn to embrace the "we" over "me" mantra.
-Chuck McCowen, Texas Elite Basketball Coach

I know you have been on the volleyball circuit for many years. In your opinion, what are the ingredients for a good player? What makes your program so effective?
"I believe a good volleyball player must learn more than just skills, they must develop good instincts while playing. A coachable player must be focused, dedicated and ready to react. You see volleyball is a lot of fun. It may look easy but it is really very challenging. Unlike many sports, volleyball is a sport in which the ball is always in motion. A player must be ready to react every second to spike, pass, serve or whatever. It takes a lot of coordination with hands, eyes, and feet.

My training style is old school. I incorporate training that improves agility, quickness, and gets players thinking through the psychology of the game. I may raise my voice and get in their face but this is done to get them to pay closer attention and be alert. I talk them through it in the moment to help them figure out before they touch the ball- what they are gonna do with the ball. My training may be viewed by some as being tough but I train players to compete at a high level. I want my middle school girl players to be ready for high school and my high school kids to be prepared to compete at college. I expect my girl players to be as aggressive as the men volleyball players— dive and attack! I run camps, skills training sessions, and my organization has club teams. Many club volleyball programs are becoming more commercialized but our program continues to strive to help each of our players become "that player". Forty percent of our club players go on to obtain college scholarships and they are prepared to compete when they get there.

Volleyball has given me so much and I've met so many good friends for over 45 years through the game. I've played and won lots of games and I've lost some. Coaching volleyball allows me to give back to the sport I love. This is the reason I have coached volleyball now for the last 26 years—it's been a way for me to pass on my experience with the game I love."

-Coach Ron Roodgari, Spike Sports Volleyball

CHAPTER 6

SUCCESS TRAINS. FAILURE COMPLAINS:
Things to Know About Physical Fitness

As we all know, physical fitness is an integral part of competitive sports. The body must be physically trained to maximize and unlock its potential.

EXERCISE REGIMENS

Coaches and trainers of every sport understand the importance of fitness training to maximize a player's performance and reduce the chance of injury. For this reason, coaches and trainers usually devise and prioritize customized fitness programs for their student athletes. Coaches work hard to ensure they strike the right balance in their physical conditioning and skills training routines while maintaining the highest regard for the safety of their athletes.

Fitness training programs usually encompass skills training as well as the following critical aspects: stretching, cardio, endurance, conditioning, speed, agility, strength, core stability, flexibility, and balance. A solid fitness training program will incorporate exercises that target these areas.

Skills Training. Skills training exercises and drills are designed to increase muscle memory and ensure proper forms and techniques are being used. Repetitive drills can help a student athlete default to automatic reactions during a game.

Stretching. Stretching is a fundamental component of physical fitness. Stretching improves blood circulation and warms up muscles and can help prevent injury.

Cardio. Cardio raises your heart rate and burns calories at a higher rate. Some cardio exercises include running, jumping rope, and cycling.

Endurance and Conditioning. Endurance and conditioning exercises increase the capacity for a student athlete to keep going with prolonged low intensity physical activities and delays the onset of fatigue. Muscular endurance means the muscles can exert a force repeatedly during a long period of time. Plyometrics and long slow runs are great workouts to improve endurance and conditioning.

Speed/Agility. Speed/agility is the time it takes to coordinate a specific movement of individual joints, or the ability to accelerate and move quickly across short distances. Using agility ladders and running high-intensity sprinting drills (called suicides) are examples of effective exercises to improve speed and agility.

Strength. Strength is the maximum force a muscle or a group of muscles together can generate against some form of resistance. Push-ups, squats, and weightlifting are some examples of helpful workout routines to build strength.

Core Stability. The core is the center of student athlete's body and encompasses the most important set of muscles. A strong core will strengthen backs, improve balance, help posture, and help avoid injury.

Flexibility/Balance. Flexibility and balance can be improved with static and dynamic exercises. Incorporating yoga into your children's workout could help increase flexibility and balance.

Yoga. Many professional athletes have tapped into this timeless form of exercise. Yoga has many proven benefits and every student athlete should consider incorporating yoga practices into their fitness regimen. It is worth exposing your children to yoga practices at any age.

Yoga targets many of the aforementioned fitness goals - increases your children's overall strength, core stability, flexibility, balance, agility, and coordination. Yoga can also help your student athlete correct muscular imbalances caused by the repetitive motion of any particular sport. Often a student athlete uses only certain muscles of their body for any given sport repetitively. Active stretching in yoga creates warmth in the body's tissue while passive stretching (holding a posture for a minute) allows muscles to lengthen even more. The result is more elastic, pliable tissue that will help your children bounce back more easily from overused and abused muscles. In essence, it helps restore balance to your children's bodies.

There are many yoga studios all around. Often they are extremely warm and welcoming to newcomers and may offer children's yoga classes separate from the adults. It is worth checking your local listings to find a yoga studio that is a good fit for your child.

ALTERNATIVE SPORTS

Consider engaging in other activities as part of your fitness regime. Alternative activities like swimming and biking are some fun and relaxing activities that can also prove to be good alternative workouts for your student athletes.

SLEEP

Sleep is a factor that cannot be overlooked in the quest to achieve optimum physical fitness. It is imperative that your children allow their body to rest to maximize their physical abilities. If your children do not get a good night's sleep, their bodies may feel impaired. Lack of sleep can cause their reactions to be slower during workouts and games. Their cognitive skills may be delayed and children may experience an overall feeling of heaviness when they are sleep deprived. So parents be sure your children learn to prioritize sleep.

The National Sleep Foundation recommends the following amount of sleep:

Child's Age	Recommended hours of sleep
06-13 years of age	9 to 11 hours
14-17 years of age	8 to 11 hours
18-25 years of age	7 to 09 hours

Remember all of these components of physical fitness are important. Every student athlete should strive to find a good balance in their pursuit to optimize their physical fitness.

CHAPTER 7
RAISE YOUR GAME:
Extra Training +More Practice +Extra Playtime = "That Player"

Any parent that has observed children playing sports has likely noticed there are some student athletes playing on a more elevated level than others. You may have wondered, "What the heck is that kid doing to get so skilled? Is it the Wheaties? Is it in the genetic makeup? Or has that kid been playing the game since birth?" More than likely, that student athlete has put in some extra work to reach that elevated level of play.

There is an expression, "Great players aren't born, they are made during the off-season." Here are some practices to help your student athletes improve their game.

Work out on their own. Have your children workout on their own. Practice after practice. Commit to a schedule, set goals, and be accountable to get better.

Skills Training. Personal training and group skills training can help develop your children's fundamentals, polish their forms, and strengthen their techniques. Group training is usually more affordable; however, personal training may offer a more customized program for your student athletes. Group training usually has a fixed schedule at a set location; whereas personal training may offer more flexibility with scheduling and location.

Whatever option you choose, try to request a trial session or sit in on a training session. Inquire about the coach's credentials, experience, availability, location etc. If it is a group training session, inquire about how many children per session usually participate in the average session. Talk to parents that have children that actually attend the training sessions. You can google search but asking other parents and coaches for referrals may prove to be more valuable. You may also check your local community gyms, recreation centers, sports leagues, or other kid - friendly sports facilities for information about group training options or personal trainers.

AAU/Elite/Club/Select Teams. AAU/Elite/Club/Select Teams offer more playtime during the off season. In theory, they should also offer a more competitive level of play. Students have an opportunity to compete within a larger pool of athletes. Furthermore, a student athlete can gain more exposure as they participate in these competitions. In certain sports, scouts frequent more of these sporting events than high school sporting events. The commitment is huge. Deciding when and if this experience is a good fit for your child is a personal choice. If you decide to go this route, you may want to consider these eight things.

1). Check experience and credentials. Check experience, credentials, coaching philosophy, and culture of the organization. You should determine if the program is a good fit for your children's needs. Make sure the program is not just about showmanship but rather development of things that matter i.e, developing solid fundamentals, personal development, and increasing IQ within that sport.

2). Consider practice location and schedules. Often practices are held 2-3 times each week so it's important that you can logistically fulfill the responsibility of allowing your children to be punctual and be in attendance. Be sure the location and practice times are conducive to your family's schedule.

3). Organization/Communication. A poorly organized program with ineffective communication, even though they may have a good coaching staff, can be a deal breaker. A pattern of last minute cancelled practices without notification; delayed updates; arbitrary increases in fees-may not be acceptable for some.

4). Parent involvement. Parent expectations may vary from one team to the next. Understand what that organization's general expectation is for each parent and make sure it's a good fit for you.

5). Skill level of team. If your children are not playing on the right level they may not get enough playing time or they may not be challenged. Be sure the skill level of the team is a good fit for your child to get the best experience possible. Inquire about opportunities to move up to play at a higher level if your child exceeds original expectations.

6). Fees /payment plans /fundraising opportunities. Fees for these programs can be expensive. Inquire about what your fees cover. Generally, the more tournaments scheduled, the more expensive the cost to join a team. Most programs offer payment schedules and may even provide fundraising opportunities. Since they are non-profit organizations you can even consider sponsorship. Be sure to inquire about all out-of-pocket costs (explicit and implied) before you make a commitment to joining an organization so that there are no financial surprises.

7). Travel teams/local teams. Local teams have limited travel expenses as they generally compete in local tournaments. Travel teams may leave the city or even the state to compete. Travel teams usually offer more exposure, but usually also have a more expensive price tag to join the team. Furthermore, traveling expenses (i.e. hotel rooms, meals, gas expenses, etc..) are typically NOT included in payment schedules. Keep in mind, if your student athletes are on travel teams, the overall expenses can add up quick. When booking hotel rooms, parents should always plan ahead to reserve rooms, inquire about all hidden charges, understand cancellation policies, and be familiar with the "stay to play" policy. "Stay to play" is an increasingly popular concept among traveling sports groups in which organizers of the competitive event require their participants use one of a selected group of pre-designated hotels. The event organizers negotiate a rebate from these hotels to help cover costs associated with their expenses. In return, the participants also benefit. In theory, this policy helps teams be able to stay together in the same hotel, ensure they are conveniently located near the event, and it locks in the room rates at a predetermined price for a specific period.

8). Tryouts. If there is a particular team your child would like to join, remember the team has to pick your child too. Many of these select/AAU/Club/Elite teams hold tryouts. If it's a team of interest, find out when they hold their tryouts and inquire about the team's available number of slots. Keep in mind some of these organizations will charge a small fee just to tryout. Your child should treat tryouts like an audition and put their very best foot forward. Mentioning their own personal accolades couldn't hurt either. Parents and student athletes should understand many of these older teams of more established programs typically have a more selective process than the younger teams. Ideally, these programs want to have children playing together at a young age and allow them to grow into the game together. In this way, the players get accustomed to playing with one another and they start to gel more while developing their fundamentals. That is a recipe for total domination. When the players reach higher levels of competition they play seamlessly and shine. This is part of the reason the competition becomes more selective for new players trying to join seasoned teams. It is not impossible, just more difficult. A new player definitely has to bring something to the table for the seasoned teams.

Training Camps. Athletic training camps offer a pocket of opportunity for development. There are usually camps being offered for various sports throughout the year during school breaks i.e., summer camps, spring break camps, back to school camps, Christmas Camps, etc. Some of these camps are sponsored by celebrities, local sports organizations, and/or schools. If you find a camp that is well organized and has good trainers facilitating the event, it could prove to be a great benefit for your student athletes. If your high school children aspire to go to a particular university, they should try to participate in sports camps sponsored by that university or camps in which the coaches/trainers from that university participate. This interaction will allow student athletes, trainers, and coaches to get to know each other better. As your children reach more elite levels of play, they may receive invitations to attend exclusive training camps that are "invitation only." These camps can also give your children an opportunity to compete with elite players and showcase their talents.

Watch Footage. Parents if you have an opportunity to record footage from games you should when possible. Your children can increase their IQ in their sport if they practice studying footage. They will see things differently watching their own performances and their teammate.

Sometimes the coaching staff makes footage available to watch, but oftentimes a parent takes the initiative to record the games.

Constructive Criticism. Encourage your children to listen to constructive feedback from their coaches and teammates. Teach your children to be receptive to receiving constructive criticism even if its delivery is not ideal. Criticism from those that know your child's game best can be good insight.

Watch YouTube instructional\Motivational Videos. Parents if you have not already discovered this convenient and powerful resource, you may be pleasantly surprised. The internet has helped level the playing field in many ways. There are so many good instructional, skills training, and motivational videos out there with top-notch trainers and great advice. Unfortunately, there is also some stuff out there with misinformation, so you must cautiously filter.

If you and your child do the research, you will likely find a YouTuber that resonates with your student athlete. They can subscribe and learn new skills or improve upon their skills. Some of these YouTubers are not only entertaining, but very motivating. They may offer great demonstrations with highly effective skills training and advice for your child's sport of choice. It can prove to be a great resource for your student athletes.

Here are just a few of my favorite YouTubers for fitness, skills training and motivation:
-ILoveBasketballTV
-Demarcus Smith ("strength no weakness")
-Ultimate Baseball Training
-Joner1on1FootballTraining
-EssentialTennislessonandInstructionforPassionatePlayers

CHAPTER 8

IT TAKES A VILLAGE:
Network with Other Parents

Parents understand if your children make the team you are also are making a serious commitment. In fact, you might need to enlist the help of your extended family. It can sometimes be a little overwhelming, especially if you have more than one student athlete. My advice, do not isolate yourself. Make it a point to get to know other parents and embrace the opportunity to form a team family.

Share information. Your child is playing the same sport as other players on the team and often you will find their interests are similar. Do not hoard information the rest of the team can also use. Every child may benefit from shared information, which in turn helps to build a better team.

Communication. Exchange emails, phone numbers, Facebook accounts, Twitter accounts, etc. This will come in handy when there is new information or last minute changes that need to be communicated quickly. Encourage everyone to use Apps like GroupMe and Team App. There are so many ways to collect conversations, share videos, score updates, and other pertinent information- embrace technology.

Pool Resources. Parents should always work together to pool their resources to find ways to support the team. Even though teams may have designated Team Moms and Team Dads-every parent should try to be involved. The general rule is the more parent involvement the better the overall experience will be for everyone. Parents should understand contributions may never be equal but contributions should always be shared. Some parents may have more time than money and vice versa. Some parents may be creative, while other parents may have a strong talent or skill in that sport. Still other parents may have connections that can prove to be valuable for fundraising and sponsorship. It's important that parents are aware of what each may bring to the table to pool resources for the optimal benefit of the team.

Rotate duties and be transparent. When handling funds parents must be honest and transparent. When assigning duties to other parents, there should be a fair rotation of duties. Implement ways to allow information to be transparent so that everyone can trust the process. Again, technology is your friend. There are sign-up programs and Apps like Sign-Up Genius to ensure volunteer list are accessible to everyone and reminders are included. This also helps ensure everyone is accountable.

Carpool. Sometimes carpooling will be essential. If your child is riding with another parent make sure you establish a check in and out process with your child. Make sure you make the effort to get to know the person your child rides with and extend the same courtesy to help out when you can. If your child is riding with another student athlete, make sure the driver is licensed and the driver's parent(s) have consented to your child being in the car.

Booster Club. Booster clubs play integral roles in the financial support of a school's sports teams and other school organizations. Booster clubs provide support through fundraising and/or coordinating events. They are usually organized and run by parents/family members of the students. The services they offer may vary from school to school. Parents support your school's booster club any way you possibly can.

CHAPTER 9
"THE BEAUTIFUL MIND":
Understanding the Coaching Culture

Coaches are usually very passionate, intense, and focused visionaries. Some coaches are volunteers, others are paid a salary. They come in all sizes, ages, colors, temperaments, personalities, and experience levels. There are no set rules that every coach follows. In fact, it is quite the contrary. Coaches usually devise and structure their programs based on their own personal philosophies about the game. When your children start with a new team, "It's like a box of chocolates." You never truly know what type of coach you are going to get. Your children's coach could range from a Phil Jackson- style (Zen is in) to the Bobby Knight-style (no holding back) or anything in between.

The most important thing to remember is most coaches will always align their actions with the team's best interest in mind. Sometimes this can prove to be in direct competition with what a parent or student athlete views as being fair. Understand most coaches are very dedicated and passionate about the game. Furthermore, coaches are very invested in the success of the team. They make unimaginable personal sacrifices for their players and their team and many coaches will go to bat for any one of their players. Parents and student athletes should understand their coach's actions may not always be easily understood. Coaches are making decisions with lots of moving pieces of the puzzle. There is a certain level of trust in the coach and the system that the players and parents MUST maintain to ensure optimal success of the team.

What issues are appropriate to raise with a coach?
There may be an occasion in which the parent or a student athlete has an issue and feels the coach needs to be approached. It could involve issues regarding practice, playtime, treatment of a player, changes in position, etc. Whatever issues you feel are important enough to raise with a

coach, make sure your issues are not petty and/or irrational. Try talking it out with another seasoned, trusted parent to get their perspective. They may be able to shine light on the matter. After conversations with others, you may come to the realization that your perspective is short-sighted.

Who should be the person talking to the coach?

If your child is very young, parents you may serve as your child's advocate. As parents, you should always strive to keep your child grounded when they express concerns involving the team and the coach. Don't be your child's "hype man" for negativity. Instead, you should strive to be objective and explain to your child the overall needs of the team may not always seem fair. Be a good listener, but also try to help them see alternative points of view. For instance, perhaps the coach rotated Monica in before Julie's serve because Julie's serve is weak and inconsistent, not because the coach doesn't like Julie. The truth can be painful sometimes to hear but should still be said. Parents, if you feel your children have valid concerns, such as mental or physical abuse, these issues should be addressed promptly and directly.

As your children grow older, parents teach them the importance of self-advocacy and diplomacy. Children need to learn to resolve their own issues, including issues with their coach. While it may be easier for you to approach the coach, it may be better for your children to do so with your guidance. Encourage your children to consult with you before approaching their coach about serious issues or concerns. In this way, you can be sure they have valid issues; give them tips on striking the right tone with the coach; and determine whether your child is even ready to have a productive, mature discussion with the coach. This is where emotional intelligence comes into play. Learning to self-advocate and be diplomatic while displaying the highest level of emotional intelligence to resolve their own issues is a critical life skill. Developing this skill early will serve your children well in sports and in life. If your student athletes master this skill, they will be sure to earn a lot of respect along the way.

So if your teenage student athlete has a concern with lack of playing time, encourage your child to have a discussion with the coach rather than intervening. For example, if your child feels they do not get enough playing time, encourage your child to approach the coach directly and ask what he/she needs to do to get more playing time. Then encourage them to do the work. Sometimes the fixes are quick fixes and other times the fixes may require a longer commitment. Allowing your children to work through their own issues verses rescuing them at every turn, will help your children in the long run. I know it can be hard to watch your children struggle and take hits, but when they master the art of regrouping on their own and getting back up for the fight — it will be a proud moment for you as a parent.

Lastly, if a majority of parents have common issues or concerns and attempts to productively talk amongst themselves have not yielded resolution, parents should arrange a parent meeting with the coach. Again, same rules apply. Parents should be courteous and respectful when requesting a meeting. Be sure to mention what the actual concerns are prior to the meeting to allow the coach an opportunity to prepare for the meeting. Make sure every parent is notified so they have an opportunity to attend the meeting if they so choose.

When to approach the coach?

Parents and student athletes should never react in the heat of the moment. Damondric Goins has over 10 years of experience coaching little league football (The Red Raiders in Freeport, TX). He explained his organization has implemented a mandatory "24 -Hour Rule." Parents are not allowed to discuss issues with coaches regarding the game for at least 24 hours after the game. Personally, I think everyone should practice establishing a cool down period to avoid a lot of unnecessary drama and hurt feelings later.

So with that said, when is the right time? Immediately before practice or immediately before and/or after a game? Probably NOT the ideal times to approach the coach. Instead, a parent or player should simply let the coach know they have a concern and request a meeting. Let the coach decide what time works best. In this way, the coach is more likely to be undistracted and the discussion can have the coach's undivided attention.

How to approach the coach?

Resist the urge to engage in negative scrutiny of the coach in front of anyone publicly. This is NEVER a good idea. Negative energy is toxic and unproductive. It can undermine the coach, cause confusion among players, and stir up resistance from other parents.

When a parent, a player, or team approaches the coach with an issue, they should always be courteous and respectful. Striking the right tone is super important. No one should approach the coach "ready for a rumble." Instead they should go in with the sincerest intentions to listen as well as be heard. Specific points should be prepared to support areas of concern with examples. It may be helpful to outline the issues beforehand to ensure the meeting stays on point. Also, when concerns are presented, you may want to incorporate "The Sandwich Method." This method incorporates criticism (the meat) between two positive comments (slices of bread). Once you have layered your issues, be ready to listen (really listen) to what the coach has to say. Remember constructive criticism goes both ways and resolution, or at least better understanding, is the ultimate goal. The coach may have a perspective you have not considered. If he or she offers criticism, be sure to listen before responding and consider what is being said. Always be prepared to offer suggestions and solutions and not just complaints.

Chain of Command.

Respect and follow the chain of command. You should always try to resolve issues with the coach directly. Usually all parties involved can be enlightened once concerns are discussed in a productive manner.

In the very rare instance, a serious issue is unable to be resolved with the coach-there are other options. If your children are participating in school sports, there is an established chain of command. When unable to resolve matters with the coach, you can request a meeting with the school's Athletic Coordinator. If you are still unable to resolve matters, the Principal of the school can then be involved. If still no resolution, the next level would be to contact the District's Athletic Director.

If your children are playing sports outside of school and you are unable to resolve important issues with a coach, you can involve the Director of that program. If that doesn't work, tough decisions may have to be made. No one wants to cause disruption to their children's athletic season; however, sometimes irreconcilable differences on critical issues may mandate a switch to another team or even organization.

Whatever the issue, I implore every parent to try to work through their differences if at all possible directly with the coach. It is usually in the best interest of all parties involved if matters can be resolved at the ground level.

CHAPTER 10

WE DON'T CALL THEM "ATHLETE STUDENTS" FOR A REASON:
Academic Success

When we use the phrase "student athlete"- the word "student" comes before "athlete" for a reason. For some student athletes academic success may come easier than others. Nevertheless, all student athletes must develop systems to ensure they are successful academically. Afterall, many institutions enforce "no pass no play." So if a student doesn't pass, they won't be eligible to play sports in school.

Here are some pointers to help your student athletes be more successful academically:

Be Organized and Prepared. Organization and preparation are essential in achieving academic success. "When you fail to plan you plan to fail." Students should practice thoroughly reading through the syllabus of every class to understand each teacher's expectations and take note of important dates for assignments and deadlines. Help your children find the best method to keep up with schedules and assignments. Student athletes can use planners or they can take advantage of the many Apps available to create schedules. Student athletes should take the time to log in important deadlines and events into their planner system and keep it updated and accurate. Students and parents should also practice checking the school-supported websites to keep up with assignments. In addition, students should make every effort to keep a clean uncluttered workspace at home and keep work organized in backpacks and/or binders. Less clutter can bring more clarity.

Time Management. Time for a student athlete is a precious thing. There are only 24-hours in a day no matter how you slice it, you can't squeeze an extra minute from a day. Successful time management is critical for student athletes to be academically successful. Teach your children good strategies for effective time management as young as possible. One strategy being, get up early and attack the day with a clear plan in mind. Student athletes should learn to set goals and decide priorities for the day- everyday. They should practice using comprehensive calendars that include all activities, assignments, workouts, games etc. Again, let technology be your friend. Your children can use Apps and planners to serve as reminders to help them stay on track throughout the day. Also, student athletes must learn NOT to overcommit themselves and avoid procrastination. Implementing some of these strategies will improve time management for student athletes, and in turn, reduce stress and allow them to get more done.

Taking Notes. Good note taking can make or break a student academically. It is imperative that your children learn to master the art of note taking to help them learn and retain information. Your children's note taking system will improve with practice. They will eventually find methods that work best for them. Here are some tips to help your student athletes improve upon this skill:

Be Prepared. Your children should get their proper rest to ensure focus is optimal. Also, be sure your children have all supplies readily accessible. If taking notes from a lecture, they should choose a seat that is distraction free and has a clear view of the board. They should also be sure they hear the lecture. If your children are taking notes while reading, make sure their environment is distraction free. Turn off electronic devices and TV. They can use the headlines within chapters as an outline for their notes as they jot down key points within each topic.

Record information. Student athletes should write all meaningful information legibly. Take "screen shots" of the board, use abbreviations to capture information quicker, and use a recording device to capture lectures if possible. Students should focus on understanding general concepts and extracting only important parts (i.e. definitions, things written on the board, headings in books, boldface words, etc.) NOT every single word has to be copied.

Summarizing Notes. Students should practice summarizing notes as soon as possible to edit information while it is fresh. They should use all the resources available to clarify meanings and relationships of ideas and concepts in their own words and make it their own. Color coordinating notes with the use of highlighters can really be effective to help emphasize points.

Reflect. Your children should think about their own opinions and ideas as they review their notes. They should try to connect information to concepts they already know and tie in the new information.

Review. Review notes frequently in smaller increments as opposed to cramming and reviewing notes just before a test.

Good Attendance and Timeliness. Learning is harder when your student athlete is missing all or part of the classroom lectures. Student athletes should strive to have good attendance and no tardies because playing catch-up due to attendance and tardiness is an unnecessary stressor. Besides, good attendance and punctuality are good habits for your children to develop in life.

Utilize Tutorials. Take advantage of tutorials at school, online and/or at learning centers. Attending tutorials offered at school will not only help students understand lessons, teachers will also recognize a student is making an effort to get help. If your child can not make school tutorials or needs more help, try searching for tutorials online. There are many free online services that are good resources. Khan Academy offers tutorials for a wide range of subjects at any level and is an excellent, comprehensive online tutorial resource. Learning centers like Sylvan Learning, Kumon, and Huntington are also great alternatives- if your child prefers face-to-face interaction. These learning centers typically provide convenient hours.

Consult with Counselors. Your children should communicate with their counselor to make sure they are on track to graduate. They should also consult with counselors to ensure they are on track to pursue a higher education and/or learn about any other career paths of interest. Counselors can assist with setting class schedules, scheduling SAT/ACT tests, reviewing requirements for admissions into various institutions and so much more.

Websites. Parents and student athletes can use websites to learn more about admission requirements for various institutions. You can visit the university's website directly or use websites like IPEDS and NCAA.

IPEDS (Integrated Postsecondary Education Data System) can be used to determine specific admission requirements for particular schools. IPEDS is a comprehensive source for information on universities, colleges, and technical and vocational schools in the United States.

NCAA provides a wealth of information for student athletes. Registering with this particular organization is beyond essential for every student athlete. It will help your child stay on track. NCAA provides a plethora of information. For example, it displays which courses, GPA, and test scores that must be met to play in Division I and Division II schools.

Texas Assured Admission Requirements charts also provide exact requirements for eligibility for institutions of higher learning in Texas. Texas House Bill 588, commonly referred to as the Top 10% Rule is a Texas law passed in 1997. This law guarantees Texas students who graduate in the top 10% of their high school class automatically get admission into all state-funded universities. Keep in mind, this Bill only guarantees admission after qualified students have submitted applications and required documents timely to the Texas school of their choice. Students must have the means to pay tuition and living expenses.

Test Taking Strategies. Good test taking strategies can go a long way in the academic success of a student. Like it or not test taking is a part of the fabric of our educational systems from beginning to end. In theory, it is a way to measure what is learned.

Here are some tips to improve your student athletes test taking skills:

1). Read instructions thoroughly. Make sure the questions are understood.

2). Be mindful of the time allotted and set a pace to answer all questions. Answer questions you are sure of first. Leave enough time to review.

3). Look for clues within the wording of questions and possible answers. Pay close attention to words like "always," "never," "except," and "all" as they may change the context of the possible answers.

4). Use deductive reasoning and the process of elimination to narrow down possible correct answers when uncertain of an answer. NEVER blindly guess.

Take College Admission Test Early. If children take the SAT/ACT test early, they can use those scores as a benchmark to determine what areas need more attention. Khan Academy offers an excellent standardized prep practice test that can help determine the areas in which your child needs more attention. Then it provides a customized review program that allows the student to concentrate their efforts on those particular areas.

Read. Read. Read. Reading increases your children's comprehension skills, vocabulary, and simply makes your children smarter. Besides, reading can prove to be a healthy distraction from other stressors in their life. Whether it's current events or for entertainment- reading can help improve the academic success of your student athlete.

CHAPTER 11
KNOW THE RULES AND EMBRACE EXPOSURE
Rules, Regulations, and Strategies for Marketing

There are rules and regulations to play any game and structures within various organizations may differ. Student athletes should understand the rules, regulations and the organizational set up of the program in which they are affiliated.

RULES, REGULATIONS, AND ORGANIZATIONAL STRUCTURES

There is structure within every sports organization and there are rules that must be followed in most every level of competition. Parents and student athletes should be familiar with the organizational structure and rules and regulations that apply to the program in which their student athletes participate. They will be held accountable for adhering to them and violations could result in a player's ineligibility or suspension.

Youth Organizations. Many youth sports organization (recreation centers, neighborhood leagues/Select/AAU/ Elite teams) will provide handbooks or have websites with information that outline their organization's policies, rules, regulations, and code of conduct for parents and players. They may also include registration requirements, fee schedules, game schedules, game rules, playtime guarantee (or not), dress codes and a ton of other useful information. I implore parents to thoroughly read any information provided as it may minimize confusion and clarify expectations throughout the season.

State school rules. Many states have their own rules for student athletes. In Texas, it's the UIL (The University Interscholastic League). The UIL governs and creates rules and administers almost all athletic contests for public primary and secondary schools in Texas. It is the largest organization of its type in the world. Many other states have similar setups and theses organizations have powerful influence over the structure of competition. For instance, in Texas the UIL arranges schools by conferences to ensure that schools compete on a regular basis with other schools in the geographic areas of a similar size. The conferences are A (the smallest), AA(2A) , AAA(3A), AAAA(4A), AAAAA(5A) and AAAAAA (the largest). Within each conference, the UIL separates the schools in regions, and then further separates the regions into districts for various contests.

UIL. The UIL is responsible for a variety of things within our schools like promoting good sportsmanship; officiating and adjudication for UIL competitions; sponsoring regional conferences and clinics for athletic competitions and so much more. Again, specific rules and regulations are laid out and failure to comply can result in ineligibility, suspension, or disqualification in a game. (You can reference UILTexas.org for more information).

NCAA. The National Collegiate Athletic Association (NCAA) is a non-profit organization which regulates athletes in over 1200 North American institutions and conferences. It also organizes the athletic programs of many colleges and universities in the United States and Canada and helps over 480,000 college student athletes who compete annually in college sports. There are currently three-division systems- Division I, Division II, and Division III. Under NCAA rules, Division I and Division II schools can offer scholarships to athletes for playing a sport. Division III schools may not offer any athletic scholarships. Generally, the larger schools compete in Division I and smaller schools in II and III.

The NCAA rules are what govern college student athletes. The NCAA rules cover a wide range of things including academic requirements, recruiting restrictions, athletic scholarships, amateurism requirements, rules of eligibility for a student transfer, and many other critical matters. Violations of NCAA rules can cause ineligibility and suspensions for college athletes.

Other. Parents and students can also learn about any other sports' organizational structures by just viewing their websites. Scrolling through an organization's website can usually provide you with a wealth of information about the organization's structure and its rules and requirements. For instance, you can visit **Olympic.org** to find out about the qualifications to participate in the Olympics.

MARKETING STRATEGIES
Undiscovered talent is more common than you may think. Not every great player will be in the limelight. With this said, marketing a student athlete's talent can improve the odds of finding a good match for their sports endeavors.

Direct Contact. Whenever you feel your children's talents are worthy to be showcased, you should consider making direct contact with coaches, recruiters, and others that can help them get to the next level. Before making direct contact, research and understand the level of expected play for your children's age or competition level. Showcasing unremarkable talents can be unproductive and/or counterproductive.

Many institutions have rules that restrict when their members can contact student athletes. For example, the NCAA rules restrict when college coaches can recruit athletes. NCAA also limits the number of "official" visits a student athlete can take to a Division I or Division II. However, there are usually no limits as far as when parents or student athletes can reach out to that institution's members.

It is common practice for parents or family members to contact coaches and recruiters about a student athlete. In fact, this is usually a common way coaches or recruiters discover talents that are not already in the limelight. Many acceptable methods of contact include email, texting, and social media. Before contacts are made, proper preparation must be made. Research must be done to make sure efforts are being directed to the right person. You must be professional, courteous, precise, and informed when reaching out. Keep in mind the person you are reaching out to may receive correspondence from lots of other people. Be sure to include a highlight video and provide instructions on how they can follow your child's athletic progress and reach out to you or your student athlete if needed. If contact is reciprocated, make sure you are familiar with the program and organization. If given the opportunity, you and your child want to be well informed so research- research-research. As mentioned previously, following key people within an organization on social media can help keep you "in the know" about the programs and organizations that are of interest to your student athlete.

Social Media Marketing. If you do not already know, social media is quickly becoming an extremely popular tool for marketing. Student athletes should consider the benefits of using social media to market their talent. Promoting your children's athletic talent on social media is smart and convenient. The reality is coaches, scouts, and recruiters are out there looking at social media accounts. It's cost effective for them too and it allows them to discover more talented student athletes.

Social media is a great platform for your children to highlight their talents but it must be used with caution and discretion. Parents remind your children everything they post may be visible to others whether it is related to sports or not. Here are some effective practices for your student athlete:

1). Establish Twitter, FaceBook, Instagram accounts and maintain an active presence.

2). Make sure account names are appropriate. Stick with a conservative, descriptive account name i.e., JohnDoe2023 (student athlete's name and year of graduation). Avoid names that may be viewed as being offensive.

3). Register with websites like NCAA, HUDL, MAXPREPS, NCSA. These websites are frequented by recruiters and will allow your children to update their stats and accolades.

NCAA: The NCAA helps to ensure eligibility requirements are met to compete for the first year of college and to potentially secure financial aid/scholarships for student athletes for Division I and Division II schools. Student athletes can create their own accounts. There is a ninety dollar fee to register. Even if you do not register, every parent and student athlete should frequent the NCAA website. They provide a wealth of information and insight for aspiring and current college athletes.

HUDL: Athletes create their own profile, share highlights, stats and scores with recruiters, friends and family. Coaches and Team Managers must sign up with HUDL and submit the names of players on their roster before players can use this service.

MAXPREPS: Maxpreps is an American website that specializes in coverage of American high school sports. It provides a very impressive source for reliable sports information. The site is owned by CBS interactive and is a division of CBS sports. It covers a range of sports i.e., football, basketball, volleyball, baseball and a variety of other sports. Maxpreps records achievements of student athletes and stats, reports scores of games, and allows student athletes and parents to share highlight videos and more.

NCSA: Next college student athletes is an athletic recruiting network that has a strong relationship to college communities. It offers help to student athletes through the recruiting process. It provides a plethora of information and support for parents, athletes, coaches and recruiters. Its mission is to help student athletes and college programs benefit from a successful recruiting process.

4). Be sure your children's social media account settings are set to public settings. This will allow coaches and other recruiters the ability to follow your student athlete and direct message them if needed.

5). Always be mindful of what is being posted and tagged on any of their accounts. Students should never post offensive and inappropriate post. Timelines should be carefully filtered and monitored to ensure anything posted is an appropriate reflection of your student athletes' values.

6). Post video highlights showcasing your children's talent. Make sure videos are short, clear, and viewers will be able to distinguish which player is your student athlete. You can use a spotlight or highlighter feature.

7). Your children should consider following trainers, coaches, and even players within the program they may be interested to stay updated on what's going on with those programs.

As always, when using social media be safe and report any suspicious activity. Do not ever post personal identifying information online (i.e., address and phone number.)

CHAPTER 12
CHOOSE A DESTINATION & MAP OUT THE ROUTE:
Explore Options and Understand the Recruitment Process

Sometimes student athletes have aspirations and the undeniable talent to compete at a higher level after high school or even before graduating from high school. This may translate into a student athletic college career, an Olympic experience, or a professional athletic sports career. The path a student athlete embarks upon is a journey that unfolds as opportunity meets hard work, dedication and preparation. Whatever the path, knowledge can help guide student athletes through their personal journey and help them make informed choices along the way.

COLLEGE PATH

A solid education can change the trajectory of future generations, or it can strengthen the solid foundation already established by previous generations. For many, the college experience will not only provide them with a good education, but it will build character and teach life lessons along the way. A college degree will also improve chances of a person having a more secure and successful career opportunity. This is the reason most parents across any ethnic, socioeconomic, and political lines would agree—a good education is one of the best ways to equip your children for success. It will prove to be a priceless asset throughout their lifetime.

Athletic Scholarships and Financial Assistance for Athletes. If your student athlete can earn a scholarship for a college education, it is a great financial benefit. Nevertheless, the reality is college athletic scholarships are awarded to less than 6% of students- that includes partial scholarships. If an athlete plans to use sports to help finance their college education, they must prepare and understand the process.

Division I. Division I schools can offer full athletic scholarships. Division I schools are the highest level of intercollegiate athletics sanctioned by the National Collegiate Athletic Association (NCAA) in the United States. DI schools include the major collegiate athletic powers, with larger budgets, more elaborate facilities and more athletic scholarships than Divisions II and III as well as many smaller schools committed to the highest level of intercollegiate competition.

Division II. Division II schools can offer "partial-scholarships." Most student athletes' college educations are funded through a mix of athletic scholarships, academic aid, need-based grants and/or employment earnings. Division II student athletes are just as competitive and in many cases just as skilled as their Division I counterparts, but institutions in Division II generally don't have the financial resources to devote to their athletic programs or choose not to place such a heavy financial emphasis on their athletic programs.

Division III. Division III schools can award need-based aid or academic-related aid to a student athlete. Academics are the primary focus for Division III student-athletes. Division III schools minimize the conflicts between athletics and academics and helps student-athletes progress toward graduation through shorter practices, playing seasons and regional competitions that take away time from academic studies. In Division III schools, student athletes are more integrated on campus with the other members of the student body. These athletes tend to be more focused on being students.

College Recruiting Process. The recruitment process is the hope of a "win-win" situation. The schools are looking for the best players they can attract and the players are looking for the best schools that will highlight their strengths while strengthening their weaknesses. Finding the right fit, on and off the court or field, is a very selective process. There are several phases of the selection process. They can be summarized as in the following stages:

1). Be Identified. Recruiting can identify talent in various ways, such as face-to-face contact, phone calls, text messages, mail, emails, or through social media. The most popular ways talented student athletes are identified are through family members and coaches. Remember you do not have to wait on coaches to reach out to you first.

2). Be Evaluated. The evaluation process involves coaches assessing the student athlete's abilities and gathering other information about them to see if they are a good fit for their program. NCAA member schools limit recruiting to certain periods during the year. Recruiting starts in June after the student's Junior year but, as mentioned, student athletes can approach coaches before then. Recruiting calendars promote the well-being of college-bound student-athletes and ensure fairness among schools by defining certain periods during the year in which recruiting may or may not occur in a particular sport. During an evaluation period, a college coach may watch college-bound student-athletes compete (high school or otherwise), visit their high schools, write or telephone student-athletes or their parents etc. During a quiet period, a college coach may not have face-to-face contact with college-bound student athletes or their parents and may not watch student-athletes compete or visit their high schools. Coaches, family members may still write or telephone on behalf of college-bound student-athletes at this time.

3). Be Engaged. This is the period in which coaches contact the student athletes personally. This may involve extending an invitation for an official visit to a college campus to college-bound student athletes or their parents. An official visit is paid for by the college. During official visits, colleges usually pay for transportation to and from the college, lodging, and three meals per day for the student athletes and their parents or guardian. They can also pay for reasonable entertainment expenses including three tickets to a home sporting events. Visits paid for by student-athletes or their parents are considered unofficial visits. During an unofficial visit, a student-athlete may only receive three tickets to a home sports event. Throughout this part of the recruitment process, the interviewing process should work both ways. Student athletes should try to find out as much about the coaches, institutions, and their programs as coaches try to find out about the student athletes. Student athletes should do their research to make a good impression regarding their knowledge of the athletic program and the institution.

4). Be Committed. Once a match is found, a verbal commitment is made. A student verbally agrees to attend an institution before signing anything.

5). Be Signed. When a student-athlete officially commits to attend a Division I or Division II school college he or she signs a National Letter of Intent, agreeing to attend that school for one academic year. Hence, this is when a college athletic career is born.

OLYMPIC OPTIONS

There are many different Olympic events. Some of the more popular Olympic sports include: track and field, gymnastics, swimming, figure skating, skiing, etc. Other not so popular Olympic sports includes: handball, canoeing, and curling. Most Olympic hopefuls must compete at high levels of competition before being invited to participate in the Olympic games. Age requirements and eligibility may vary according to the sport.

Qualification for the Olympics is controlled by the International Olympic Committee (IOC) and international sporting federations. Qualifications are different for every sport. To maximize global participation, there are quotas for various regions and caps are placed on the number of participants from any one country in each event. Eligible athletes are then nominated by the national sporting federations. There are various approaches to selecting an Olympian. Some sports hold tryouts and others use subjective judgements of an athlete's performance to make selections. Final selections are usually made by the country's designated

Olympic Committee. A selected athlete must sign the Team Agreement to take their place in the Olympic Games. You can visit **Olympic.org** for more information.

OTHER OPTIONS

Fewer than 2% of NCAA players go on to play professional sports. If there is an alternative option your student athletes may be interested in pursuing someday, I encourage you to research and review that pathway with your children so they understand what the journey may entail. Are there age eligibility requirements? Would they have to travel? What are the salary ranges?

Although the government has set standards for minors to be employed only with written consent under the age of sixteen, many leagues (minor or major) have adopted minimum age requirements and education requirements that may restrict young athletes from being eligible from participation even if their athletic talents say otherwise. It has been a long debated issue, as many believe some players are unfairly prevented from cashing in on their talents at a young age- no matter how talented they are and no matter how much they may need the income.

Here are some requirements for professional sports players:

National Football League (NFL). The NFL does not have a minimum age requirement for professional football players; however, the NFL mandates that a player must be out of high school for at least three years before they are eligible to play in the NFL.

Arena Football League (AFL). The AFL's minimum age requirement to play arena football is 18 years old. Players must be in optimal physical fitness and must try out and be selected by an AFL team.

National Basketball Association (NBA). The NBA requires a player be at least 19 years of age during the calendar year of the draft. The player must have completed basketball eligibility at an American high school and must also be at least one year removed from the graduation of his school class.

International Basketball Leagues. No Education Required. Typically discovered in high school and college games. Salaries are unremarkable compared to NBA salaries but salaries and incentives could be negotiated as a player gains more popularity.

Major League Baseball (MLB). The basic categories of players eligible to be drafted into the MLB are as follows: high school players that have graduated from high school and have not yet attended college or a junior college; college players from a four-year college who have either completed their junior or senior years or are at least 21 years of age or junior college players (regardless of how many years of school they completed).

When your student athletes are all grown up and they still want an outlet to play sports, they are likely to find a good fit if they look for it. Parents remind your children there are a wide variety of options out there. They do NOT have to stop playing a sport they love to play if they DO NOT make it to a professional level of play. Whether they choose to play for competition, workout, or just for fun! There are many outlets to choose from that may appeal to various levels of commitment and competition levels i.e., adult recreational sports leagues, church leagues, and sports leagues through work. Remind them there are undeniable health benefits that can be reaped if they continue engaging in some level of sports activities throughout their lifetime.

CHAPTER 13
Becoming.

Statistically speaking, only a very small percentage of students will earn a full college scholarship for athletics and an even more minuscule number will have a professional athletic career playing sports. However, many of our student athletes will become future healthcare workers, lawyers, educators, business owners, military servicemen/servicewomen, politicians, coaches, and maybe parents someday. The journey of a student athlete will equip them for greatness in whatever path their lives take far after they play their last game. They will be disciplined, hardworking, confident, and resilient. They will know the importance of being a good leader as well as a good team player when they enter the workforce and when they have their own families.

Parents know that all of your sacrifices and investments in your children's journey as student athletes will help propel them into successful directions in their lives. Every moment of their student athletic experience will contribute towards tapping into their inner greatness! Every practice, every game, every dropped pass, every buzzer-beating goal, every blow out, every pep talk —every single experience while playing sports (good, bad, or indifferent) will contribute to your children **becoming** the very best version of themselves possible.

I pray blessings over your journey with your student athletes. You are all deserving of the highest honor as MVP—**Most Valuable Parents**!

Professional References:

Toya Anderson
Dr Kathleen Cullinane, Chiropractor
Coach Damondric Goins, Red Raiders Little League Football
Coach Armando Gonzalez. H.S. Coach
Dr. Monica Robinson Green
Coach D. King, Drills=Skills
Chuck McCowain, Texas Elite AAU Basketball
Coach Melynda McGregor, H.S. Coach
Coach Johnnie Means, Harris County Aquatics Commissioner
Genevieve Robinson
Coach Ron Roodgari, Spike Sports Volleyball
Dr. Tammye Turner
Fred Washington, Prairie View A&M Athletics Director

CTESociety.org
KidsHealth.org
NCAA.org
Olympic.org
SleepFoundation.org
TexasKidsFirst.org
UILTexas.org

The Solar Body: The Secret to Natural Healing by Ilchi Lee

Special Thanks to my personal MVP Village:

Dawn Burton

Alexandria Chi

LaTrece Curry

Gloria Dail

John Dewey

LaDawn Fletcher

Ann Frazier

Margaret Frazier

Keisha Foxworth

Veronica Guzman

Karen Lufsey

Keri Johnson

Monique Johnson

Janice MacArthur

Earl Melebeck

Felton Nails

Stephaine Rainey

Christopher Tabron

Tanya Watkins

*Coach Ware & The Warriors in Missouri City, TX

*Coach Simon & The Lady Vikings in SugarLand, TX

Made in the USA
Middletown, DE
22 December 2021